RICH
ON ANY
INCOME

RICH
ON ANY
INCOME

*The Easy Budgeting
System That Fits
in Your Checkbook*

James P. Christensen and Clint Combs
with George D. Durrant

SHADOW MOUNTAIN
Salt Lake City, Utah

The information in this book is revised and updated from time to time. For information about recent changes, write to Christensen & Combs, Inc., 4525 South 2300 East, Suite 202, Salt Lake City, Utah 84117.

Library of Congress Cataloging-in-Publication Data

Christensen, James P.
   Rich on any income.
     1. Finance, Personal. I. Combs, Clint. II. Durrant,
George D. III. Title.
   HG179.C565   1985   640'.42   85-22222
   ISBN 0-87597-009-7 (pbk.)

Printed in the United States of America   18961-4678
20 19 18 17 16 15 14 13 12 11

Contents

Preface

Our business is helping people solve their financial problems. Almost always, financial problems have little to do with how much money you make. We once counseled an executive who was making $200,000 a year. He was nearly bankrupt, and his marriage was crumbling because of the stress caused by the fact that he and his wife did not know how to live on his salary. An elementary school principal we know was in danger of having her sports car repossessed. She felt like a complete failure because she had overextended herself in her personal debt.

No matter what your income, financial freedom is essential if you are to have an overall sense of well-being. And financial freedom comes not from having a large income, but from managing the income you have. Careful money management, or the lack thereof, can tip your emotional scale toward happiness or misery.

Our years of experience in counseling thousands of individuals and couples have taught us over and over again that financial freedom is always part of the ground upon which happy people stand. Those in financial bondage are enslaved by circumstances that hold them bound to misery.

The vast majority of women's worries are related to money problems. Nearly 89 percent of all divorces occur because the couples could not deal with the pressures related to their family finances.

A Bold Promise

Based on the experiences that we and the other personnel of Christensen & Combs Corporation have had in working with over 50,000 people from all walks of life, we can without hesitation make this bold promise: We promise you that by faithfully following the principles and procedures set forth in this book, you can set out on a road that will ensure your future financial security and will bring you the joy and peace that come as you gain and maintain your financial freedom.

In fact, we *guarantee* that if you follow this method sincerely and carefully, you will be living within your means in ninety days. Now, this doesn't mean that your house will be paid for, that your car will be paid for, or that educational loans or other necessities will all be wiped off the slate. But by following the simple system in this book, you will experience the thrill of seeing how all of these debts can be taken care of, and at the same time you will be walking into the light of financial freedom.

To reap the benefits of this promise, you must firmly resolve to follow the system for at least ninety days, and you should decide now exactly when you will start. If you are married, you and your spouse must also commit to each other that you will follow this plan for ninety days. The first month you will learn the system; the next month you will love it; and the third month it will become an integral part of your life. After ninety days, using the system will have become spontaneous, and you will have formed a habit that will keep you out of financial bondage for the rest of your life. Is it worth ninety days of your time? Forgive us for asking such a ridiculous question.

1

The Financial Freedom Budgeting System

You can be rich on any income by using the Financial Freedom Budgeting System, which is a simple way for you to manage your budget in your checkbook in seven seconds per financial transaction.

This simple budgeting tool is shown here, and you will find some actual budget booklets in the back of this book.

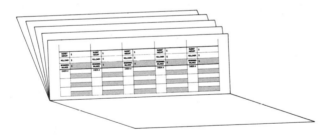

How does this tool work? First, you take the total of your monthly income and divide it into twenty-five or fewer budget categories. (We'll say more about how to do that later in the book.) Then you list each of the allocated amounts in one of the twenty-five columns in the budget booklet. For example, in a spending category you have labeled *groceries,* you might list the amount of $315.

Now you are ready to head to the grocery store. You have your checkbook (including your check register and your blank checks), and you have also inserted your budget booklet into your checkbook.

As you select your groceries, you mentally note the portion of the month still remaining and the number of dollars left in your grocery budget as recorded in the budget booklet. This will enable you to not deplete the remaining amount of allocated grocery money before the end of the month. You then proceed with your cart to the checkout stand. The clerk says, "That will be $62.37." You proceed in the usual manner to write out a check to the store for $62.37. As you always do, you record the transaction in your check register and subtract the amount of the check from your previous balance.

But now you do something new—something that will require only seven additional seconds and that will put you in control of your money. You turn to the page of your budget booklet that has the "groceries" column, and in that column you write down the check number and the amount, $62.37. You subtract that figure from the remaining amount left in the "groceries" column for that month, $315. That leaves $252.63 still available for groceries until the end of the month. The next time you purchase groceries, you do the same thing. And, of course, you handle the other spending categories in a similar manner. By doing this, you will know at all times exactly where you have spent your money and how much you have left to spend in any budget category.

This system is powerful, but it is also simple. There are no complicated papers to carry with you, and there is no complicated bookkeeping to do at home. You can now keep track of your budget in seven extra seconds right in the store, at the service station, or wherever you write out a check.

This system is not overwhelming, as other budgeting systems are. Any man, woman, or child can, with little effort, understand, follow, and benefit from it.

As you read on, you will see how couples can harmonize two checkbooks into one system. You will learn how to use this budgeting system to make credit cards a positive tool rather than a nagging problem. You will learn how to handle emergency spending without having a financial disaster. You will learn how to save a year's supply of money. You can do it, and when you do, you will be rich on any income.

We've now given you a brief overview of how the Financial Freedom Budgeting System works and of what it will do for you. Let's back up now and look at the system from front to back. In other words, let's get you started on the road to financial freedom.

2

Getting Started

Financial difficulties are caused by one or more of the following problems:
1. Lack of financial planning.
2. No systematic method for financial control.
3. Impulse buying and lack of sales resistance.
4. Illusions that somehow financial problems will go away.

Let's look at actual cases of each of these problems.

Lack of Financial Planning

Jim and Judy both worked, Jim as a successful lawyer and Judy as the secretary to the high-school principal. Their combined income seemed far more than adequate for them and their two teenage daughters.

Because of a desire to live in a manner Jim described as "free," they lived without worrying about budgeting. "After all," Jim said, "we earn enough to get what we want without always worrying about pinching pennies like my parents did."

But things were not working out. Jim blamed their financial problems on inflation and bad luck in the stock market. Judy didn't know what was wrong and often told her best friend that she and Jim had found out that money doesn't buy happiness. The more they earned, the less they seemed to have. The constant strain to pay the endless bills was emotionally draining to her and was causing considerable discord between her and Jim.

No Systematic Method for Financial Control

Valerie had spent fourteen years with a computer firm. She had risen through the ranks to a fine position in middle management.

She lived in an apartment with her well-mannered cat.

Because she lived alone (other than the cat) and because her eating habits were simple, her food budget was small. And her needs in other areas were far from extravagant. The great mystery of her life was, as she put it, "What is happening to my money?"

She was living well and had nice things to wear and a beautiful car. She was paying her bills as they came in. She kept track of her checks and always knew what her bank balance was. Unfortunately, it was often near zero.

She wanted to help her younger brother, who was a sophomore in college, but she just couldn't seem to find money to do it. Her plan to save money for a down payment on a condominium was an unfulfilled dream.

Impulse Buying and Lack of Sales Resistance

Karl and Liz's money problems had them on the verge of disaster. Karl worked as a maintenance man at the hospital. They lived in a humble home just a block from the hospital. The payments on the home were well within their meager means.

Their problem was the grocery store. They loved to eat. The whole family went together to shop. Each child liked a certain brand of breakfast cereal, and each chose his own. Karl loved to watch television, but he needed a lot of snack food to really be able to enjoy his favorite shows and ball games.

Liz was attractive and often received compliments on looking so young and trim. She felt that clothes were the key to her appearance. She couldn't seem to pass up a store where new blouses hung in the window. Payday often sent her downtown.

"She looks great," Karl said, "but if she doesn't slow down on spending, she'll have us bankrupt."

Illusions That Somehow Financial Problems Will Go Away

Pam felt that if Rick would face reality they could solve their money problems. All she could get out of him when he purchased a second shotgun was, "Come on honey, duck hunting is no fun without you along."

When she reminded him of their financial plight, his reply was, "You worry too much. We've made it this far. Things will get better—just watch and see."

Until Jim and Judy, Valerie, Karl and Liz, and Pam and Rick learn to solve their financial problems, they will be in financial bondage. And the same is true of you.

The Financial Freedom Budgeting System outlined in this book will:

1. Help you formulate a financial plan.
2. Give you a systematic method for financial control.
3. Give you control over impulse buying.
4. Make your financial problems go away.

The Financial Freedom Budgeting System is made up of four parts, which are shown on this diagram.

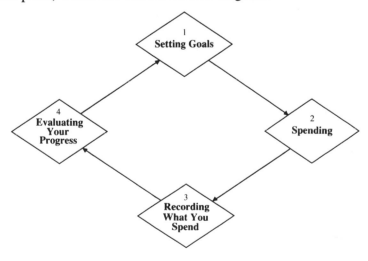

Setting Goals

Setting budgeting goals is simple. You merely match your expenditures to your income. You decide how to distribute your income among what you will purchase during the month, such as food, clothes, entertainment, and transportation. We'll show you how to do this later on.

Much of the rest of this book is devoted to showing you not only how to define your goals and objectives, but how to crystalize them in writing.

It has been said, "Where performance is measured, performance improves." Writing your goals down allows you to measure your performance so you can improve.

Spending

Spending is the most entertaining part of your budget. There are two forms of spending, positive spending and negative spending. Positive spending is spending according to the goals you have set. Negative spending is spending on impulse. When you spend on impulse, you're not getting the highest and best use out of your money—most items bought on impulse could have been purchased elsewhere for less, and many of these things need not have been purchased at all.

Recording What You Spend

This book will give you a unique system for recording what you spend. It requires only a few seconds each time you write out a check, and it will give you complete and constant control over your finances.

Evaluating Your Progress

The next step is to evaluate your progress. We suggest that you do this weekly for the first three months, reviewing your goals and spending patterns from the written record. If you are married, do this with your spouse. The first ninety days will be the hardest, but after that rather grim initial period, you'll find a certain joy attached to this self-discipline. When you sit down and review your goals and your spending, you will experience the joy that comes from controlling your expenditures rather than having them control you.

3

Becoming Committed

For any budgeting system to work, you must be committed
to it. The principle of commitment is well expressed in this
story about an aged emperor and his court:

The emperor called in all of his magicians, high lamas, and
seers, and said, "I'm getting old, and my time as your emperor
fades fast. Before I depart, I wish to learn all the wisdom of
mankind. As your emperor, I commission you to go out and
search throughout the world and bring back to me the wisdom
of all the ages."

Respecting the emperor's wishes, these important men of
the kingdom took this great responsibility and went throughout
the world seeking the greatest wisdom of the ages.

After a year of research, they came back with sixteen
scrolls of information. They said to the emperor, "O most honorable emperor, live forever. Here within these sixteen scrolls
you will find the wisdom of all of the ages of mankind."

The emperor looked at the huge scrolls and said, "I'm getting old, and my eyes are getting dim. Can you reduce it to one
scroll?"

The men went back, worked diligently, and, finally, came
back with one scroll.

The emperor said, "That is still too big. Can you reduce it
to one sheet?"

The men worked on it diligently and reduced it to one sheet. Then, after many months, they came back.

The emperor said, "I'm now incapable of reading, but my understanding is great. Can you reduce it to one line?"

This was a difficult challenge for the wise men of the kingdom, but they were finally able to reduce the wisdom of the ages down to one line. Then they reported to the emperor.

They said, "O most honorable emperor, live forever. We now have the wisdom of all the ages of mankind contained in one line so that you may remember before your death what this great wisdom is."

The emperor excitedly said, "Tell me the wisdom of all the ages in one line."

The wise men replied, *"There ain't no such thing as a free fortune cookie!"*

How does the point of that story apply to financial management? To gain financial freedom, you must be committed to follow the system explained in this book—you must pay the price. It won't always be easy, but we guarantee it can be done, and you can do it.

4

Calculating Income and Expense

The first step in using the Financial Freedom Budgeting System is to estimate your monthly income for the next twelve months. Let's use an example of someone who earns a gross income of about $2,000 a month. If we subtract federal, state, and Social Security taxes, that will leave a net spendable monthly income of about $1,740.

Estimated Monthly Income.

Gross income
per month $ 2,000

Taxes   (120)
FICA   (140)
                   ——————
Net Spendable $ 1,740

If you are salaried, you probably already know your monthly income. If you receive commissions, use your average monthly commission based on the past twelve months. As an example, if last year you had average commissions of $2,000 a month and you know this year you are doing better, you would set up your budget on what you have actually earned in commissions in the past twelve months, that is, $2,000. Anything you receive over those commissions, you can put into savings.

Now calculate your net spendable income by subtracting federal, state, and Social Security taxes, and any other deductions from your gross income.

Estimated Monthly Income

    Gross income

    per month   _____

    Taxes   _____

    FICA   _____

Net Spendable _____

That's how much you can spend each month. That seems obvious, but many of us quickly forget that fact. You can spend less, but if you spend more, then you are in trouble.

The next step is to calculate your average monthly expenditure for the past twelve months. Let's take an example of one couple we worked with. The chart below shows how this couple spent their average monthly spendable income for the past twelve months. You will note that this couple spent an average of $1,609 a month in twenty different categories. (Use the "Sample Budget Builder" on page 76 to plan your own expenditures.)

CATEGORY	MONTHLY TOTAL
1. Allowances	35
2. Automobiles	210
3. Cleaning and laundry	7
4. Clothing	35
5. Contributions	210
6. Debt payments	
7. Family Advancements	27
8. Gifts	25
9. Groceries	285
10. Housing	475
11. Insurance	20
12. Investments	
13. Maintenance and improvements	22
14. Medical, dental, drugs	20
15. Miscellaneous, petty cash	20
16. Recreation and entertainment	35
17. Savings	30
18. Subscriptions	8
19. Utilities	100
20. Vacation, trips	45
	1,609

If you look at item 9, groceries, you will see that it is $285 a month. How did this couple come up with that average? They added up the amount they had spent on groceries during the past twelve months. The total was $3,420. They divided this by twelve to calculate an average monthly expenditure of $285.

Your assignment now is to calculate your average monthly expenditures for the past twelve months. Take every canceled check, every credit-card invoice, every cash receipt that you have, and then sort them into categories similar to the ones in the example. As you do this, you should eliminate all one-time expenditures from your average monthly expenditure for the past twelve months so you don't overinflate your spending average. Examples of one-time expenditures would be recarpeting a room, reroofing your home, purchasing a large appliance, and buying new tires.

You will probably come up with different categories than we used in our example. Some families like to divide their expenditures into twelve categories. Others use as many as twenty-five. The average is about nineteen. Remember, you must determine what you define each of the categories to mean. For example, when you buy groceries, do you just buy groceries? Or do you purchase toothpaste, beauty aids, paper products, and medicines as part of your grocery budget?

Once you get the total spent for each category for the past twelve months and have divided it by twelve, you can use that figure as a basis in calculating your average monthly expenditure in each category for the next twelve months. You can do this in one of two different ways. The first way is what we call the *projection method*.

The projection method is really an educated guess as to what your expenses will be. Let's say that last year you spent $285 a month for groceries. To determine what you will spend during each month of the coming year, you might think, "Last year my average monthly expenditure on groceries was $285. This year I think because of rising costs I am probably going to spend $325 each month.

If you would like to be a little more precise, you can use the second method, which is called the *inflation factor method*.

Using this method, you take the average monthly expenditure of the past twelve months and multiply it by 110 percent. This will increase your average monthly expenditures for the next twelve months by 10 percent to guard against inflation. It will give you a financial cushion while you are learning to budget effectively. In the example, multiplying $285 by 110 percent would give us about $315.

Whichever method you choose, if you anticipate any one-time expenditures like a new television, you should determine the cost, divide it by twelve, and add it to an appropriate category, such as maintenance and improvements.

CATEGORY	LAST 12 MONTHS	X	PROJECTED OR INFLATION FACTOR	=	NEXT 12 MONTHS
1. Allowances	35				40
2. Automobiles	210				235
3. Cleaning and laundry	7				10
4. Clothing	35				40
5. Contributions	210				230
6. Debt payments					
7. Family Advancements	27				30
8. Gifts	25				25
9. Groceries	285				315
10. Housing	475				475
11. Insurance	20				20
12. Investments					
13. Maintenance and improvements	22				25
14. Medical, dental, drugs	20				20
15. Miscellaneous, petty cash	20				20
16. Recreation and entertainment	35				40
17. Savings	30				40
18. Subscriptions	8				10
19. Utilities	100				115
20. Vacation, trips	45				50
	1,609				1,740

If calculating your expenses over the past year seems overly difficult, we would encourage you to simply sit down and guess at reasonable figures for the different categories. The most important thing is that you begin using the system, and you can always make refinements later.

5

Pruning the Spending Tree

In the example we have been using, average monthly expenditures have increased from $1,609 to $1,740. Fortunately, this is exactly the amount of take-home pay in the example.

But what if that was not the case? This couple would then be like the average American family or individual. Let's say that they projected that they would spend $1,920. In that case, they would be going into the hole $180 a month. That would be a nightmare. What could they do to avoid this disastrous condition?

Here are six different steps that you can use to make your average monthly expenditures for the next twelve months equal your net spendable income for the next twelve months.

First, look at your budget and evaluate all of your fixed expenditures. What is it that you *must* legally pay? You probably have to pay the utilities, house payment, car payment, and so on. We refer to these as fixed expenditures. These items are those that cannot be altered.

Next, look at variable expenses. These are expenses that are needed but over which you do have some control, such as clothing, food, music lessons, and so forth. In each case, you can cut back if you have to. After you have adjusted these categories, add them to your fixed expenditures. Now do things balance better? If not, read on.

Expenses such as recreation and entertainment are called discretionary expenses. Such expenses are one of the highest spending areas in any budget and are emotionally the most difficult to reduce. But these expenses are ones over which you have almost total control. To balance your budget, they must sometimes be sacrificed. When you have completed listing your fixed expenditures, adding to them your variable and discretionary expenditures, and reducing where you can, if your budget is still in the red, there are several things you can do.

One thing you can do is to visit your bank (the one where you have a loan) and tell them that you would like to reamortize or consolidate your debt service, or in other words, that you would like to extend your loan or combine all your loans into only one payment to reduce your monthly payments to a level you can afford. Most banks are willing to extend or consolidate your credit. They would rather have your principal and interest than repossess your washing machine. If you decide to consolidate your loans, make sure that your new payment is lower than all your previous loan payments combined. If it isn't, you need to reamortize, not consolidate your debt service.

If you are in serious financial difficulty, you may have to sell something to get your income to equal your outgo. Perhaps you could sell a piece of land, a car, a boat, or ski equipment. If you have to sell an asset that you really love, not only will it bring you more money so that you can solve your financial problems, but it will give you the incentive to discipline yourself in your quest for financial freedom. Even if you have to sell something you love, by using the Financial Freedom Budgeting System, you will be able to replace it when you are financially free.

In very rare cases, declaring personal bankruptcy is the only way to escape financial bondage. If you are considering bankruptcy, you should seek competent professional legal counsel before doing so.

Of course, you may also be able to meet all of your expenses by finding a way to increase your income. You may be able to find a second job, work in the evening from your home, or start a small business. You may be able to get a raise from your present employer. Or perhaps you can find a different job that pays more than the job you have now. There are many possibilities if you will take time to find them, evaluate them, and act upon them.

This chart shows a summary of what we've just said.

What to do if your projected expenses are larger than your income

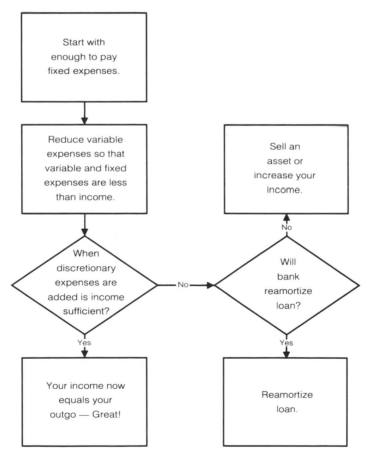

6

Sharing the Burden
and the Joy

Both single and married people can have money problems.
However, marriage adds complications, so if you are married,
it is essential that you and your spouse have a weekly financial
planning meeting in which you review your available income,
analyze your past expenditures, and plan for the coming week.
The key to the success of such meetings is to agree that you will
not condemn each other for mistakes you have made in spending during the past week. You must have "instant forgiveness."
Don't worry about who spent what or didn't keep track of this
or that. Just instantly forgive any errors you feel your spouse
has made. Then go on to plan what you will do in the week to
come. If you follow this procedure, over time you will see
things begin to improve in your financial situation and in your
communication with each other.

The next step in developing your budget is to decide how
you and your spouse will share your financial responsibility. To
do this, simply divide the responsibility for the categories between the two of you. Decide which one of you will be respon-
sible for each category.

If you are single, of course, you get to handle all the
categories by yourself.

We have found that when only one person in a marriage is
handling all of the financial responsibility, there is no com-

munication or sharing. In such cases resentment and mistrust may quickly follow.

By sharing the financial responsibility, you will find that financial burdens become lighter, you will be happier, and your communication on financial matters will become an enriching experience.

You can see in the chart below that the husband handles the house payment and the wife handles maintenance and improvements. Utilities are paid by the husband. Both share the automobile expenses, and so on down the line until all the spending categories are assigned. (Use the "Sample Budget Builder" on page 76 to plan your own expenditures.)

CATEGORY	AVERAGE EXPENDITURES FOR NEXT 12 MONTHS	HIS	HERS
1. Allowances	35	✓	✓
2. Automobiles	210	✓	✓
3. Cleaning and laundry	7		✓
4. Clothing	35		✓
5. Contributions	210	✓	
6. Debt payments		✓	
7. Family Advancements	27		✓
8. Gifts	25		✓
9. Groceries	285		✓
10. Housing	475	✓	
11. Insurance	20	✓	
12. Investments			
13. Maintenance and improvements	22		✓
14. Medical, dental, drugs	20		✓
15. Miscellaneous, petty cash	20		✓
16. Recreation and entertainment	35	✓	
17. Savings	30	✓	
18. Subscriptions	8		✓
19. Utilities	100	✓	
20. Vacation, trips	45	✓	
	1,609		

Once you have decided who will pay what, you write in the numbers from your average monthly expenditure for the next twelve months. (See the chart below.) When you add up the figures in the example, you see that the husband is going to manage $1,185, and the wife is going to manage $555.

CATEGORY	AVERAGE EXPENDITURES FOR NEXT 12 MONTHS	HIS	HERS
1. Allowances	35	√ 20	√ 20
2. Automobiles	210	√ 195	√ 40
3. Cleaning and laundry	7		√ 10
4. Clothing	35		√ 40
5. Contributions	210	√ 230	
6. Debt payments		√	
7. Family Advancements	27		√ 30
8. Gifts	25		√ 25
9. Groceries	285		√ 315
10. Housing	475	√ 475	
11. Insurance	20	√ 20	
12. Investments			
13. Maintenance and improvements	22		√ 25
14. Medical, dental, drugs	20		√ 20
15. Miscellaneous, petty cash	20		√ 20
16. Recreation and entertainment	35	√ 40	
17. Savings	30	√ 40	
18. Subscriptions	8		√ 10
19. Utilities	100	√ 115	
20. Vacation, trips	45	√ 50	
	1,609	1,185	555

Next, go to your bank and set up two separate checking accounts, one for you and one for your spouse in joint ownership.

Two separate accounts make it easier to avoid the chaos that can come from uncoordinated bank withdrawals.

The husband's account should have his name first and his wife's name second. The wife's account should have her name first and her husband's name second. In case of emergencies, each should be able to sign the other's checks.

7

Using the
Financial Freedom
Budget Booklet

After you have divided up responsibility for the different spending categories and have set up separate checking accounts, the next step is to conveniently lay out your expenses into an organized system. The budget booklet we have for doing that is the best ever devised. It is simple and easy to use, and yet it always lets you know exactly where you stand. You will find copies of this booklet at the end of this book. Follow the instructions on how to assemble the booklets.

Now take out your checkbook and insert the Financial Freedom Budget Booklet between your check register and your checks. This illustration shows how this booklet fits into your checkbook.

You will notice as you open the booklet that there is a place for five spending categories; turn the page, and there are five

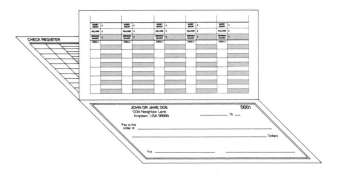

more; turn again and there are five more. Keep turning, and you will find that there are twenty-five in all. This will be more than you will usually need.

Below is an example of how to begin using the budgeting booklet. (This example is of a couple. If you are single, the system is even easier to use.) You can see how the *his* account is set up at the beginning of each month. We will explain how to use the rollover section of the budgeting booklet later.

RECORD ALL CHARGES OR CREDITS THAT AFFECT YOUR ACCOUNT

NUMBER	DATE	DESCRIPTION OF TRANSACTION	PAYMENT/DEBIT (-)	√ T	FEE (IF ANY) ( )	DEPOSIT/CREDIT (+)	BALANCE
						$	$ 1740 00
1	1/1	Hers	$ 555 00		$	$	555 00
							1185 00

	Hers		House		Auto		Contributions		Miscellaneous
BUDGET AMOUNT	$ 555.00	BUDGET AMOUNT	$ 590.00	BUDGET AMOUNT	$ 195.00	BUDGET AMOUNT	$ 230.00	BUDGET AMOUNT	$ 170.00
ROLLOVER	$	ROLLOVER	$	ROLLOVER	$	ROLLOVER	$	ROLLOVER	$
BEGINNING BALANCE	$ 555.00	BEGINNING BALANCE	$ 590.00	BEGINNING BALANCE	$ 195.00	BEGINNING BALANCE	$ 230.00	BEGINNING BALANCE	$ 170.00
CHECK # 1	555.00	CHECK #		CHECK #		CHECK #		CHECK #	
	.00								

You can see that the husband's account shows categories for his wife, the house, auto, contributions, and miscellaneous. These total to $1,740, which is his allotment of the couple's total spendable income. In the check register, he records the check to his wife's account for her January allotment in the amount of $555. He subtracts this amount from his bank balance, leaving $1,185.

Next, he turns to the Financial Freedom Budget Booklet and under the *hers* category subtracts check number 1 for $555. This leaves a zero balance in this category. Then he turns to his checkbook and writes out a check for $555, which he gives to his wife to deposit in her account.

In this example, all of the income for the family is being funneled through the *his* account to the *hers* account. You can also funnel the income from the *hers* account to the *his* account if you choose. By using this procedure, you will find that managing your budget is orderly and simple.

Now, let's look at the wife's account. She deposits the check into her account and records it in her check register as illustrated, carrying the balance forward.

RECORD ALL CHARGES OR CREDITS THAT AFFECT YOUR ACCOUNT

NUMBER	DATE	DESCRIPTION OF TRANSACTION	PAYMENT/DEBIT (-)	√ T	FEE (IF ANY) (-)	DEPOSIT/CREDIT (+)	BALANCE	
			$		$	$	$	00
	1/1	Me					555	00
		January				555 00	555	00

She then turns to her Financial Freedom Budget Booklet and allocates her budget as follows:

Maintenance	$ 25
Auto	$ 40
Groceries	$315
Clothing	$ 50
Miscellaneous	$125

Maintenance		Auto		Groceries		Clothing		Miscellaneous	
BUDGET AMOUNT	$ 25.00	BUDGET AMOUNT	$ 40.00	BUDGET AMOUNT	$ 315.00	BUDGET AMOUNT	$ 50.00	BUDGET AMOUNT	$ 125.00
ROLLOVER	$	ROLLOVER	$	ROLLOVER	$	ROLLOVER	$	ROLLOVER	$
BEGINNING BALANCE	$ 25.00	BEGINNING BALANCE	$ 40.00	BEGINNING BALANCE	$ 315.00	BEGINNING BALANCE	$ 50.00	BEGINNING BALANCE	$ 125.00
CHECK #		CHECK #		CHECK #		CHECK #		CHECK #	

She now has a $555 balance in her check register and Financial Freedom Budget Booklet. It is important that the figures in the check register and the budget booklet balance.

When the wife goes shopping, she writes out check number 1 to Safeway for groceries in the amount of $75. In her check register, she subtracts out the $75 and has $480 left in her checking account. Immediately after, she goes to her Financial Freedom Budget Booklet and, under *groceries,* places the check number in the box, subtracts the $75 from her allotment of $315, and has $240 left.

RECORD ALL CHARGES OR CREDITS THAT AFFECT YOUR ACCOUNT

NUMBER	DATE	DESCRIPTION OF TRANSACTION	PAYMENT/DEBIT (-)	√T	FEE (IF ANY) (-)	DEPOSIT/CREDIT (+)	BALANCE $
							00
	1/1	Me	$		$	$	555 00
		January				555 00	555 00
1	1/4	Safeway					75 00
		Groceries	75 00				480 00

Maintenance		Auto		Groceries		Clothing		Miscellaneous	
BUDGET AMOUNT	$ 25.00	BUDGET AMOUNT	$ 40.00	BUDGET AMOUNT	$ 315.00	BUDGET AMOUNT	$ 50.00	BUDGET AMOUNT	$ 125.00
ROLLOVER	$	ROLLOVER	$	ROLLOVER	$	ROLLOVER	$	ROLLOVER	$
BEGINNING BALANCE	$ 25.00	BEGINNING BALANCE	$ 40.00	BEGINNING BALANCE	$ 315.00	BEGINNING BALANCE	$ 50.00	BEGINNING BALANCE	$ 125.00
CHECK #		CHECK #		CHECK #	75.00	CHECK #		CHECK #	
				1	240.00				

By keeping track of her spending in this way, she will always know at a glance how much she has left in her budget in each of the spending categories. She can shop more wisely and plan more carefully. She can plan her expenditures by looking forward, rather than looking back at what she has already spent.

Check number 2 is for gasoline. It is made out to Texaco for $20. You can see that it is subtracted from her check balance of $480, leaving her $460. In the Financial Freedom Budget Booklet under *auto*, she subtracts out the $20, leaving $20 for gas expenses for the rest of the month.

RECORD ALL CHARGES OR CREDITS THAT AFFECT YOUR ACCOUNT

NUMBER	DATE	DESCRIPTION OF TRANSACTION	PAYMENT/DEBIT (-)	√T	FEE (IF ANY) (-)	DEPOSIT/CREDIT (+)	BALANCE $
			$		$	$	00
	1/1	Me				555 00	555 00
		January					555 00
							75 00
1	1/4	Safeway	75 00				480 00
		Groceries					
							20 00
2	1/8	Texaco	20 00				460 00
		Gas					

Maintenance		Auto		Groceries		Clothing		Miscellaneous	
BUDGET AMOUNT $	25.00	BUDGET AMOUNT $	40.00	BUDGET AMOUNT $	315.00	BUDGET AMOUNT $	50.00	BUDGET AMOUNT $	125.00
ROLLOVER $		ROLLOVER $		ROLLOVER $		ROLLOVER $		ROLLOVER $	
BEGINNING BALANCE $	25.00	BEGINNING BALANCE $	40.00	BEGINNING BALANCE $	315.00	BEGINNING BALANCE $	50.00	BEGINNING BALANCE $	125.00
CHECK #		CHECK # 2	20.00 20.00	CHECK # 1	75.00 240.00	CHECK #		CHECK #	

Check number 3 shows a purchase of shoes and a small part for the television. The total of the check is $25. This again is subtracted from the balance, leaving $435 in the bank account. In the Financial Freedom Budget Booklet, she subtracts $10—which was the television part—from the maintenance column, leaving $15, and from the clothing column she subtracts the $15 for shoes, leaving $35 for clothes. This way you can write out one check and divide it between two or more categories.

RECORD ALL CHARGES OR CREDITS THAT AFFECT YOUR ACCOUNT

NUMBER	DATE	DESCRIPTION OF TRANSACTION	PAYMENT/DEBIT (-)	√T	FEE (IF ANY) (-)	DEPOSIT/CREDIT (+)	BALANCE
			$		$	$	$ 00
	1/1	Me					555 00
		January				555 00	555 00
1	1/4	Safeway	75 00				75 00
		Groceries					480 00
2	1/8	Texaco	20 00				20 00
		Gas					460 00
3	1/14	Penney's	25 00				25 00
		Shoes and TV part					435 00

Maintenance		Auto		Groceries		Clothing		Miscellaneous	
BUDGET AMOUNT	$ 25.00	BUDGET AMOUNT	$ 40.00	BUDGET AMOUNT	$ 315.00	BUDGET AMOUNT	$ 50.00	BUDGET AMOUNT	$ 125.00
ROLLOVER	$	ROLLOVER	$	ROLLOVER	$	ROLLOVER	$	ROLLOVER	$
BEGINNING BALANCE	$ 25.00	BEGINNING BALANCE	$ 40.00	BEGINNING BALANCE	$ 315.00	BEGINNING BALANCE	$ 50.00	BEGINNING BALANCE	$ 125.00
CHECK # 3	10.00 15.00	CHECK # 2	20.00 20.00	CHECK # 1	75.00 240.00	CHECK # 3	15.00 35.00	CHECK #	

Check number 4 in the check register again is for groceries, in the amount of $90. The wife subtracts $90 from her bank balance, leaving $345. She also deducts this from the Financial Freedom Budget Booklet, leaving $150 for groceries for the rest of the month. Note here that she did not necessarily have to make out the check for the exact amount of the food purchased. For example, the groceries may have cost only $50, but she could have written the check for $90, keeping $40 in cash for later small grocery purchases such as a loaf of bread or a carton of milk.

Check number 5 is to Mr. Jones for Bill's piano lessons. Again she subtracts it from her balance, leaving $335, and then deducts it from her miscellaneous balance in the budget booklet, leaving $115 in that category.

RECORD ALL CHARGES OR CREDITS THAT AFFECT YOUR ACCOUNT

NUMBER	DATE	DESCRIPTION OF TRANSACTION	PAYMENT/DEBIT (-)	√ T	FEE (IF ANY) (-)	DEPOSIT/CREDIT (+)	BALANCE $	00
	1/1	Me	$		$	$	555	00
		January				555 00	555	00
		Safeway					75	00
1	1/4	Groceries	75 00				480	00
		Texaco					20	00
2	1/8	Gas	20 00				460	00
		Penney's					25	00
3	1/14	Shoes and TV part	25 00				435	00
		Food King					90	00
4	1/15	Groceries	90 00				345	00
		Mr. Jones					10	00
5	1/18	Piano Lessons	10 00				335	00

Maintenance		Auto		Groceries		Clothing		Miscellaneous	
BUDGET AMOUNT	$ 25.00	BUDGET AMOUNT	$ 40.00	BUDGET AMOUNT	$ 315.00	BUDGET AMOUNT	$ 50.00	BUDGET AMOUNT	$ 125.00
ROLLOVER	$	ROLLOVER	$	ROLLOVER	$	ROLLOVER	$	ROLLOVER	$
BEGINNING BALANCE	$ 25.00	BEGINNING BALANCE	$ 40.00	BEGINNING BALANCE	$ 315.00	BEGINNING BALANCE	$ 50.00	BEGINNING BALANCE	$ 125.00
CHECK # 3	10.00	CHECK # 2	20.00	CHECK # 1	75.00	CHECK # 3	15.00	CHECK # 5	10.00
	15.00		20.00		240.00		35.00		115.00
				4	90.00				
					150.00				

Check number 6 for $25 again goes to Texaco to buy gasoline. Subtracting that from her bank balance, our heroine has $310 left. She subtracts $25 from the budget booklet auto column, and what does she find? She is $5 in the hole (oops). She spent $5 more than she budgeted for it. But the system still lets her maintain control; at least she knows how much she has overspent, whereas before, she never really knew until the end of the month. Later we will show you what to do if you over-spend.

Checks numbers 7 and 8 are handled in the same way as the previous checks.

RECORD ALL CHARGES OR CREDITS THAT AFFECT YOUR ACCOUNT

NUMBER	DATE	DESCRIPTION OF TRANSACTION	PAYMENT/DEBIT (-)	√T	FEE (IF ANY) (-)	DEPOSIT/CREDIT (+)	BALANCE
			$		$	$	335 00
6	1/20	Texaco	$		$	$	25 00
		Gas	25 00				310 00
7	1/22	Cash and Carry					115 00
		Groceries	115 00				195 00
8	1/27	Zale's					15 00
		Marsha's wedding	15 00				180 00

Maintenance		Auto		Groceries		Clothing		Miscellaneous	
BUDGET AMOUNT	$ 25.00	BUDGET AMOUNT	$ 40.00	BUDGET AMOUNT	$ 315.00	BUDGET AMOUNT	$ 50.00	BUDGET AMOUNT	$ 125.00
ROLLOVER	$	ROLLOVER	$	ROLLOVER	$	ROLLOVER	$	ROLLOVER	$
BEGINNING BALANCE	$ 25.00	BEGINNING BALANCE	$ 40.00	BEGINNING BALANCE	$ 315.00	BEGINNING BALANCE	$ 50.00	BEGINNING BALANCE	$ 125.00
CHECK # 3	10.00	CHECK # 2	20.00	CHECK # 1	75.00	CHECK # 3	15.00	CHECK # 5	10.00
	15.00		20.00		240.00		35.00		115.00
		6	25.00	4	90.00			8	15.00
			(5.00)		150.00				100.00
				7	115.00				
					35.00				
	15.00		(5.00)		35.00		35.00		100.00	= 180.00

At this point in our example, it is the end of the month. The wife brings down all of the remaining balances from each of the categories in the Financial Freedom Budget Booklet. She still has $15 in maintenance. She has overspent $5 for auto. And she has $35 left in her grocery budget, $35 left in her clothes budget, and $100 left in miscellaneous for a total of $180. What does she do with this $180? What would you do? Spend it, right? No, you would handle it by using what we call the *rollover system*. In our last illustration, at the end of January, $35 was left for groceries. Using the rollover system, you would take the $35 and add it to your grocery budget ($315) for February. So in the grocery column in your February budget booklet you would have $350.

If you look at the illustration below, you will see that we have started a new booklet for the month of February before completing the rollover. At the very top, you would place "Maintenance," "Auto," "Groceries," "Clothing," and "Miscellaneous" as your budget categories for February. The "budget amount" would be your actual expenditures for each of the next twelve months, which you calculated earlier. You would put $25 under "Maintenance," $40 under "Auto," $315 under "Groceries," $50 in "Clothing," and $125 in "Miscellaneous."

Then, in the "Rollover" section of the booklet, you would put *what is left* from the month of January. In this case, we have + $15 under "Maintenance," − $5 under "Auto," + $35 under "Groceries," + $35 under "Clothing," and + $100 under "Miscellaneous." Now you would add to (or subtract from) the rollover amounts from the previous month your original budget amounts to get a new "Beginning Balance" for February. Your beginning balances for the new month would be $40 under "Maintenance," $35 under "Auto," $350 under "Groceries," $85 under "Clothing," and $225 under "Miscellaneous." Now you are ready to begin a new month.

January

	Maintenance	Auto	Groceries	Clothing	Miscellaneous
BUDGET AMOUNT	$ 25.00	$ 40.00	$ 315.00	$ 50.00	$ 125.00
ROLLOVER	$	$	$	$	$
BEGINNING BALANCE	$ 25.00	$ 40.00	$ 315.00	$ 50.00	$ 125.00
CHECK #	3 10.00	2 20.00	1 75.00	3 15.00	5 10.00
	15.00	20.00	240.00	35.00	115.00
		6 25.00	4 90.00		8 15.00
		(5.00)	150.00		100.00
			7 115.00		
			35.00		
	15.00	(5.00)	35.00	35.00	100.00

= 180.00

February

	Maintenance	Auto	Groceries	Clothing	Miscellaneous
BUDGET AMOUNT	$ 25.00	$ 40.00	$ 315.00	$ 50.00	$ 125.00
ROLLOVER	$ 15.00	$ (5.00)	$ 35.00	$ 35.00	$ 100.00
BEGINNING BALANCE	$ 40.00	$ 35.00	$ 350.00	$ 85.00	$ 225.00
CHECK #					

You should record your original budget on the cover of the budget booklet each month for future rollovers. This will regularly remind you of your original category amounts.

What about that $5 that was overspent in the auto category in January? Subtract $5 from your auto budget in February. This will help you to see where your budget is unrealistic. We will explain how to adjust your overall budget later.

At the beginning of a new month, you must make sure that the balance in your check register and in your Financial Freedom Budget Booklet are the same. We call this the *balancing rule*. To find out if your check register and budget booklet balance, simply add up the beginning amounts in all the columns of the budget book at the beginning of the month. Then compare it with the balance in your check register at the beginning of the month. In the example, the budget-book categories add up to $735. This balances with the amount in the check register, which is also $735.

RECORD ALL CHARGES OR CREDITS THAT AFFECT YOUR ACCOUNT

NUMBER	DATE	DESCRIPTION OF TRANSACTION	PAYMENT/DEBIT (-)	√T	FEE (IF ANY) (-)	DEPOSIT/CREDIT (+)	BALANCE
			$		$	$	$ 335 00
6	1/20	Texaco	25 00				25 00
		Gas					310 00
7	1/22	Cash and Carry	115 00				115 00
		Groceries					195 00
8	1/27	Zales	15 00				15 00
		Marsha's wedding					180 00
	2/1	Me				555 00	555 00
		February					735 00 √

	Maintenance		Auto		Groceries		Clothing		Miscellaneous
BUDGET AMOUNT	$ 25.00	BUDGET AMOUNT	$ 40.00	BUDGET AMOUNT	$ 315.00	BUDGET AMOUNT	$ 50.00	BUDGET AMOUNT	$ 125.00
ROLLOVER	$ 15.00	ROLLOVER	$ (5.00)	ROLLOVER	$ 35.00	ROLLOVER	$ 35.00	ROLLOVER	$ 100.00
BEGINNING BALANCE	$ 40.00	BEGINNING BALANCE	$ 35.00	BEGINNING BALANCE	$ 350.00	BEGINNING BALANCE	$ 85.00	BEGINNING BALANCE	$ 225.00
CHECK #		CHECK #		CHECK #		CHECK #		CHECK #	

Everything you write in your check register must also be included in your budget booklet. And everything you write in your budget booklet must be included in your check register. That way, you will always be in balance. For an example, see how checks 9, 10, and 11 have been handled in the following illustration.

RECORD ALL CHARGES OR CREDITS THAT AFFECT YOUR ACCOUNT

NUMBER	DATE	DESCRIPTION OF TRANSACTION	PAYMENT/DEBIT (-)	√T	FEE (IF ANY) (-)	DEPOSIT/CREDIT (+)	BALANCE
							$ 335 00
6	1/20	Texaco / Gas	25 00		$	$	25 00 / 310 00
7	1/22	Cash and Carry / Groceries	115 00				115 00 / 195 00
8	1/27	Zales / Marshas Wedding	15 00				15 00 / 180 00
	2/1	Me / February				555 00	555 00 / 735 00
9	2/2	Alpha Beta / Food-90, Craft-10	100 00				100 00 / 635 00
10	2/6	ABC TV / TV repair	45 00				45 00 / 590 00
11	2/6	American / Gas	20 00				20 00 / 570 00

Maintenance		Auto		Groceries		Clothing		Miscellaneous	
BUDGET AMOUNT	$ 25.00	BUDGET AMOUNT	$ 40.00	BUDGET AMOUNT	$ 315.00	BUDGET AMOUNT	$ 50.00	BUDGET AMOUNT	$ 125.00
ROLLOVER	$ 15.00	ROLLOVER	$ (5.00)	ROLLOVER	$ 35.00	ROLLOVER	$ 35.00	ROLLOVER	$ 100.00
BEGINNING BALANCE	$ 40.00	BEGINNING BALANCE	$ 35.00	BEGINNING BALANCE	$ 350.00	BEGINNING BALANCE	$ 85.00	BEGINNING BALANCE	$ 225.00
CHECK # 10	45.00 (5.00)	CHECK # 11	20.00 15.00	CHECK # 9	90.00 260.00	CHECK #		CHECK # 9	10.00 215.00

After you have used the budgeting system a few months, you will probably find it necessary to adjust the amounts budgeted for the different categories. In fact, we recommend that you do review these figures every three months and adjust them as necessary. For example, you may find that you are consistently spending more in the auto category and less in the clothing category than you had budgeted. If so, you would need to increase the amount budgeted for auto and decrease the amount budgeted for clothing. Your needs will change over time, and you will need to adjust your budget figures accordingly. Of course, you will not increase your overall budget (unless your income increases). You will simply adjust the amounts within the categories to reflect your actual spending habits.

As you can see, this method of budgeting is simple and effective, and you can begin using it now to manage your own finances.

As you have seen in previous examples, one booklet represents a month of expenditures. But how do you use the booklet if you get paid twice a month, weekly, or even more often? To keep things simple, we suggest that each booklet should represent a pay period with its corresponding budget figures. If you get paid once a month, you would need only one booklet a month; if you get paid twice a month, you might want to use one booklet for the first pay period and then start a second one for the second pay period. Or, if you get paid weekly, you might want to use a new booklet every single week.

Another way to handle this is to build up your savings to equal a month's net income and then fund your monthly budget from your savings. You would use only one budget booklet a month in this case. Then, every time you receive your paycheck, you would deposit it into your savings. Each month you would withdraw from your savings what you need to fund your budget for the month.

We believe that the simpler your system, the easier you will find it to manage your money. Choose the system that works best for you.

On the cover of your booklet are columns labeled "First Paycheck" or "His," and "Second Paycheck" or "Hers." (See the illustration below.) The First Paycheck and Second

Paycheck columns are for people who get paid more than once a month or who have different paychecks at different times of the month. By using these columns for every pay period, you can decide which categories each check will cover. Or, if you wish, you can also use these columns to show who will handle which categories. You can't use the columns both ways at the same time, however.

Notice that the budget categories on the cover of the booklet are slightly shaded. If you have a spending category that isn't the same as one listed, just write it over the shaded printing of one of the categories you don't use. You can list up to five additional categories in the blank spaces provided.

CATEGORY	AMOUNT	FIRST PAYCHECK OR HIS	SECOND PAYCHECK OR HERS	CATEGORY	AMOUNT	FIRST PAYCHECK OR HIS	SECOND PAYCHECK OR HERS
1. Allowances	$			13. Maintenance & improvements	$		
2. Automobiles	$			14. Medical, dental, drugs	$		
3. Cleaning & Laundry	$			15. Miscellaneous, petty cash	$		
4. Clothing	$			16. Recreation & entertainment	$		
5. Contributions	$			17. Savings	$		
6. Debt payments	$			18. Subscriptions	$		
7. Family advancements	$			19. Utilities	$		
8. Gifts	$			20. Vacation trips	$		
9. Groceries	$			21.	$		
10. Housing	$			22.	$		
11. Insurance	$			23.	$		
12. Investments	$			24.	$		
				25.	$		

NAME _____ MONTH _____ YEAR _____   TOTAL $ _____ _____ _____

8

Controlling Credit-Card Purchases

You can hardly buy anything in this country without a credit card. The battle cry of millions of Americans is "Charge it." Then they make themselves sick trying to pay the bills that inevitably come. But, using the Financial Freedom Budget System, you can control the plague of plastic money.

We recommend using only one credit card for personal needs and one for business. Then use your personal card only in emergencies, which do happen. One of our clients was traveling between Evanston and Laramie, Wyoming. Between those two towns there are not many people and even fewer cars, and she had a mechanical failure. Fortunately, a tow truck came along. She didn't have enough cash to pay him, and he would not accept a check, but her credit card solved the problem. Credit cards are sometimes necessary.

How do you handle credit-card purchases with the Financial Freedom Budget System? There are two ways. Both are easy to do. Most important, they will help you handle your credit-card purchases properly and safely.

The first way: When you use your credit card to purchase an item, record the transaction just as you would if you had written a check.

However, instead of writing the check number in the check number area, draw a box, as in the illustration, around the check number area in your check register. We refer to this box as the *magic box*. It's magic because it keeps you out of credit-card debt; it helps you save money and stop worrying about whether you will have any money when the credit-card bill arrives.

Let's use an example. Suppose that on February 8 you went to Nordstrom's and bought some clothes for $40. You would record the purchase in your check register and draw a box around the check number area. In your Financial Freedom Budget Booklet, you would record the transaction as usual, but you would also draw a box around the check- number area here.

RECORD ALL CHARGES OR CREDITS THAT AFFECT YOUR ACCOUNT

NUMBER	DATE	DESCRIPTION OF TRANSACTION	PAYMENT/DEBIT (-)	√ T	FEE (IF ANY) ( )	DEPOSIT/CREDIT (+)	BALANCE $ 570 00
MC	2/8	Nordstroms	$		$	$	40 00
		Mom's clothes	40 00				530 00

	Maintenance		Auto		Groceries		Clothing		Miscellaneous
BUDGET AMOUNT	$ 25.00	BUDGET AMOUNT $ 40.00		BUDGET AMOUNT $ 315.00		BUDGET AMOUNT $ 50.00		BUDGET AMOUNT $ 125.00	
ROLLOVER	$ 15.00	ROLLOVER $ (5.00)		ROLLOVER $ 35.00		ROLLOVER $ 35.00		ROLLOVER $ 100.00	
BEGINNING BALANCE	$ 40.00	BEGINNING BALANCE $ 35.00		BEGINNING BALANCE $ 350.00		BEGINNING BALANCE $ 85.00		BEGINNING BALANCE $ 225.00	
CHECK # 10	45.00	CHECK # 11	20.00	CHECK # 9	90.00	CHECK # MC	40.00	CHECK # 9	10.00
	(5.00)		15.00		260.00		45.00		215.00

In both boxes you would then put the initials of the credit card that you used. For example, if you used your MasterCard, you would put the initials MC in the lower part of the box. If you used your VISA, you would put the initial V in the box. For American Express, you would use the initials AE. And so on. This lets you know which cards you used and which ones you need to pay.

Now, when your credit-card bill arrives, how do you handle it? In this illustration, we are assuming that you charge some clothing at Nordstrom's with your MasterCard on February 8 and that the bill comes in that same month to be paid. (Actually the bill would arrive the following month, but this way we can show you more clearly what to do.)

You have received your MasterCard bill for your purchase of $40 at Nordstrom's. Let's suppose that the bill includes a $5 service charge. (The service charge or interest would probably not be that high, but it gives us an easy figure to work with.) On February 25 you get out your checkbook and write check number 16 for $45 to MasterCard. You record the check in your check register and circle the check amount. This identifies the check as a special check that was written to pay a credit-card bill.

RECORD ALL CHARGES OR CREDITS THAT AFFECT YOUR ACCOUNT

NUMBER	DATE	DESCRIPTION OF TRANSACTION	PAYMENT/DEBIT ( )	√ T	FEE (IF ANY) ( )	DEPOSIT/CREDIT (+)	BALANCE	
			$		$	$	570	00
MC	2/8	Nordstroms / Mom's clothes	40 00				40 00	
							530	00
12	2/10	Safeway / Groceries	85 00				85	00
							445	00
	2/13	Mom / Gift from Uncle				50 00	50	00
							495	00
13	2/20	Texaco / Gas	20 00				20	00
							475	00
14	2/21	Food King / Groceries	135 00				135	00
							340	00
15	2/21	Winchell's Donuts / Church activity	60 00				60	00
							280	00
16	2/25	Master Charge / Bill plus 5.00	(45 00)				5	00
							275	00

Next, you subtract $5 (not $45) from the balance in your check register. Why did you subtract only $5? Because you have already subtracted the $40 that you charged at Nordstrom's. This is identified by the square around the check-number area. So, all that is left to deduct is the $5 service charge. Then, you must also deduct the service charge from the miscellaneous column in the budget booklet as shown.

RECORD ALL CHARGES OR CREDITS THAT AFFECT YOUR ACCOUNT

NUMBER	DATE	DESCRIPTION OF TRANSACTION	PAYMENT/DEBIT ( )	√ T	FEE (IF ANY) ( )	DEPOSIT/CREDIT (+)	BALANCE $ 570	00
MC	2/8	Nordstroms	$		$	$	40	00
		Mom's clothes	40 00				530	00
12	2/10	Safeway					85	00
		Groceries	85 00				445	00
	2/13	Mom					50	00
		Gift from Uncle				50 00	495	00
13	2/20	Texaco					20	00
		Gas	20 00				475	00
14	2/21	Food King					135	00
		Groceries	135 00				340	00
15	2/21	Winchell's Donuts					60	00
		Church activity	60 00				280	00
16	2/25	Master Charge					5	00
		Bill plus 5.00	(45 00)				275	00

Maintenance		Auto		Groceries		Clothing		Miscellaneous	
BUDGET AMOUNT	$ 25.00	BUDGET AMOUNT	$ 40.00	BUDGET AMOUNT	$ 315.00	BUDGET AMOUNT	$ 50.00	BUDGET AMOUNT	$ 125.00
ROLLOVER	$ 15.00	ROLLOVER	$ (5.00)	ROLLOVER	$ 35.00	ROLLOVER	$ 35.00	ROLLOVER	$ 100.00
BEGINNING BALANCE	$ 40.00	BEGINNING BALANCE	$ 35.00	BEGINNING BALANCE	$ 350.00	BEGINNING BALANCE	$ 85.00	BEGINNING BALANCE	$ 225.00
CHECK # 10	45.00	CHECK # 11	20.00	CHECK # 9	90.00	CHECK # MC	40.00	CHECK # 9	10.00
	(5.00)		15.00		260.00		45.00		215.00
		13	20.00	12	85.00			2/13	50.00
			(5.00)		175.00				265.00
				14	135.00			15	60.00
					40.00				205.00
								16	5.00
									200.00

In this example, you subtracted the $5 service charge from the miscellaneous column. However, as you calculate your average monthly expenditure at the end of the year and find that most of your credit-card purchases were for clothing, you might decide that next year you will subtract the finance charges from the clothing category rather than the miscellaneous category. This could apply to any category where major purchases are made with a credit card.

If the bill would have been for only $40 with no finance charge, you would have recorded a zero in your check register and brought down the balance of $280.

Next, you should record the number 16 in the top part of the boxes in your check register and budget booklet. That tells you the Nordstrom's purchase for $40 was paid with check number 16 and recorded in the register and budget booklet.

RECORD ALL CHARGES OR CREDITS THAT AFFECT YOUR ACCOUNT

NUMBER	DATE	DESCRIPTION OF TRANSACTION	PAYMENT/DEBIT ( )	√ T	FEE (IF ANY) ( )	DEPOSIT/CREDIT (+)	BALANCE $
			$		$	$	570 00
16 MC	2/8	Nordstroms Mom's clothes	40 00				40 00 530 00

Another way to handle credit cards is to set up a budget category titled "Credit-Card Purchases."

Again suppose you have made a purchase from Nordstrom's for $40 for clothing using your MasterCard.

Note that the categories are the same except for "Credit-Card Purchases" (abbreviated "Cr Cd Purchases").

After making the purchase, start with the budget booklet, not the check register. Under "Clothing," make the magic box. Then subtract the $40 purchase as before. Under "Cr Cd Purchases," place +$40 in the white space and bring down the balance of +$40. "Budget Amount," "Rollover," and "Beginning Balance" would have all zeroes unless you rolled over any balance of this category for which you have not written a check to pay your credit-card bill.

Using this option, you do not fill out your check register until the bill arrives. Why? Because you are accumulating the amounts of the purchases in your new budget category. When the bill comes, you write only one check for all the purchases and then fill out your check register. Then under "Cr Cd Purchases," you write a −$40 to clear out that category.

Maintenance		Auto		Groceries		Clothing		Cr Cd Purchases	
BUDGET AMOUNT	$ 25.00	BUDGET AMOUNT	$ 40.00	BUDGET AMOUNT	$ 315.00	BUDGET AMOUNT	$ 50.00	BUDGET AMOUNT	$ 0
ROLLOVER	$ 15.00	ROLLOVER	$ (5.00)	ROLLOVER	$ 35.00	ROLLOVER	$ 35.00	ROLLOVER	$ 0
BEGINNING BALANCE	$ 40.00	BEGINNING BALANCE	$ 35.00	BEGINNING BALANCE	$ 350.00	BEGINNING BALANCE	$ 85.00	BEGINNING BALANCE	$ 0
CHECK # 10	45.00	CHECK # 11	20.00	CHECK # 9	90.00	CHECK # MC	40.00	CHECK #	+ 40.00
	(5.00)		15.00		260.00		45.00		40.00
		13	20.00	12	85.00			16	− 40.00
			(5.00)		175.00				0
					135.00				
				14	40.00				

We once spoke to a group of young married couples who had just purchased their first homes. Many of the couples said something like this: "We have five credit cards, and we used each of them up to the limit. We have $10,000 worth of credit-card bills. How can we ever get rid of those?"

If you are in a similar situation, you can pay off your credit-card balances by making a separate category, "Past Credit-Card Payoff." Every month, pay off a little of your balance until it is all paid. However, for this to be effective, you must not use your credit cards anymore, and now that you are using the budget system, you should not have to. So, in our opinion, one of the best things you can do is destroy all credit cards except your emergency card and promise your-self that you will never get into credit-card debt again.

If you make purchases with a bank card, you will not record them the way you record credit-card purchases. With a bank card, there is no future billing—the money is deducted directly from your checking account. So, you can treat bank card purchases much as you would those made with a check, but instead of recording a check number, record the initials BC (for "Bank Card").

9

Making a Deposit

Let's look at how to record bank deposits in your check register and budget booklet. You will notice that there are two deposits on our check register in the illustration. We will discuss only the first; the second is for your review. Let's assume that you receive a gift of $50 and deposit it in your checking account. Where the check number would go in the check register, you leave a blank. You write in the date (in this case February 13) and record the deposit of $50. Then you add it to your balance, now totaling $495.

RECORD ALL CHARGES OR CREDITS THAT AFFECT YOUR ACCOUNT

NUMBER	DATE	DESCRIPTION OF TRANSACTION	PAYMENT/DEBIT (-)	√ T	FEE (IF ANY) (-)	DEPOSIT/CREDIT (+)	BALANCE
							570	00
16 MC	2/8	Nordstroms Mom's clothes	$ 40	00		$	$	40	00
							530	00
12	2/10	Safeway Groceries	85	00				85	00
							445	00
	2/13	Mom Gift from Uncle				50	00	50	00
							495	00
13	2/20	Texaco Gas	20	00				20	00
							475	00
14	2/21	Food King Groceries	135	00				135	00
							340	00
15	2/21	Winchell's Donuts Church activity	60	00				60	00
							280	00
16	2/25	Master Charge Bill plus 5.00	45	00				5	00
							275	00
	2/25	Me Refund for Winchell's Donuts	$		$	$ 60	00	60	00
							335	00
17	2/28	Sports House John Keds	20	00				20	00
							315	00

Next, you go to the miscellaneous column in the budget booklet and put the date (February 13) in the check-number area. Then you record your deposit of $50 and add it to your balance, and you have $265 left to spend.

Maintenance		Auto		Groceries		Clothing		Miscellaneous	
BUDGET AMOUNT	$ 25.00	BUDGET AMOUNT	$ 40.00	BUDGET AMOUNT	$ 315.00	BUDGET AMOUNT	$ 50.00	BUDGET AMOUNT	$ 125.00
ROLLOVER	$ 15.00	ROLLOVER	$ (5.00)	ROLLOVER	$ 35.00	ROLLOVER	$ 35.00	ROLLOVER	$ 100.00
BEGINNING BALANCE	$ 40.00	BEGINNING BALANCE	$ 35.00	BEGINNING BALANCE	$ 350.00	BEGINNING BALANCE	$ 85.00	BEGINNING BALANCE	$ 225.00
CHECK # 10	45.00 (5.00)	CHECK # 11	20.00 15.00	CHECK # 9	90.00 260.00	CHECK # 16 MC	40.00 45.00	CHECK # 9	10.00 215.00
		13	20.00 (5.00)	12	85.00 175.00	17	20.00 25.00	2/13	50.00 265.00
				14	135.00 40.00			15	60.00 205.00
								16	5.00 200.00
								2/25	60.00 260.00

If you wish, you could divide the $50 among several categories, for example, putting $10 under miscellaneous, $20 under clothes, and $20 under groceries. You can distribute those deposits in any way you see fit. Using this system, you are in constant control of your finances.

10

Balancing Your Checkbook

Let's suppose that it is the beginning of a new month. You have totaled the columns in your budgeting booklet and made sure that they equal the balance in your check register. And you have received your bank statement in the mail and are ready to reconcile your checkbook with the statement.

To balance the check register, go through the following procedure with each check. Let's take check number 9 as an example. First, verify the information that you wrote on the check with what you recorded in your check register. You would say to yourself, "The check was to Alpha Beta for $90 in food and a $10 gift. The total was $100, which I placed in the check column and subtracted it from my balance. In the budget booklet under groceries, I subtracted $90 from $350 and brought down my balance of $260. Then I went over to the miscellaneous column and subtracted $10 from the $225 for a balance of $215. This all agrees with the check register, and the budget booklet, and the canceled check." After you have completed this step of reconciliation, you put a check mark in the column by the $100 check amount as illustrated.

RECORD ALL CHARGES OR CREDITS THAT AFFECT YOUR ACCOUNT

NUMBER	DATE	DESCRIPTION OF TRANSACTION	PAYMENT/DEBIT (-)	√ T	FEE (IF ANY) ( )	DEPOSIT/CREDIT (+)	BALANCE
			$		$	$	$ 335 00
6	1/20	Texaco	25 00				25 00
		Gas					310 00
7	1/22	Cash and Carry	115 00				115 00
		Groceries					195 00
8	1/27	Zales	15 00				15 00
		Marshas Wedding					180 00
	2/1	Me				555 00	555 00
		February					735 00
9	2/2	alpha Beta	100 00	√			100 00
		Food-90, Crpt-10					635 00
10	2/6	ABC TV	45 00				45 00
		TV repair					590 00
11	2/6	American	20 00				20 00
		Gas					570 00

Maintenance		Auto		Groceries		Clothing		Miscellaneous	
BUDGET AMOUNT	$ 25.00	BUDGET AMOUNT	$ 40.00	BUDGET AMOUNT	$ 315.00	BUDGET AMOUNT	$ 50.00	BUDGET AMOUNT	$ 125.00
ROLLOVER	$ 15.00	ROLLOVER	$ (5.00)	ROLLOVER	$ 35.00	ROLLOVER	$ 35.00	ROLLOVER	$ 100.00
BEGINNING BALANCE	$ 40.00	BEGINNING BALANCE	$ 35.00	BEGINNING BALANCE	$ 350.00	BEGINNING BALANCE	$ 85.00	BEGINNING BALANCE	$ 225.00
CHECK # 10	45.00	CHECK # 11	20.00	CHECK # 9	90.00	CHECK # 16 MC	40.00	CHECK # 9	10.00
	(5.00)		15.00		260.00		45.00		215.00
		13	20.00	12	85.00	17	20.00	2/13	50.00
			(5.00)		175.00		25.00		265.00
				14	135.00			15	60.00
					40.00				205.00
								16	5.00
									200.00
								2/25	60.00
									260.00

A natural question would be, "If I have subtracted eleven of my credit-card purchases out of my balance column in the check register, when the bank statement comes to be reconciled, won't the balance be off because I have recorded my credit-card purchases before I have actually paid them?"

Yes, it will. To make everything balance, you will need to add back to the balance in your check register the credit-card purchases that you have not yet actually paid for. This additional amount should easily balance your checkbook each month.

11

Saving Your Surplus

After using the budgeting system for a few months, you should be spending less than you earn, and you will want to start saving the surplus. This is wise, for many people don't save anything. A national news network stated that a third of American families have no savings. And only half could pay an unexpected bill of $1,000. We feel this is not because they can't save; it's because they don't know how. But now you do, and we recommend that you save 10 percent of your gross income every month.

You may be thinking you can't save even 3 percent. If so, consider the elephant theory of savings. Saving money is like eating an elephant—you can't do it in one bite. Instead, you have to bite off a little at a time. Try saving just 1 percent of your income. When you feel comfortable with that, go to 2 percent. Keep building until you can save a full 10 percent.

Don't try to go from 3 percent to 8 percent, for example, in one giant bite. If you do, you might choke. Just move slowly but steadily until you reach your goal.

We suggest dividing your savings into three categories. If you save $200 a month, put 60 percent, or $120, into permanent savings. Use this money to purchase investments to increase your net worth and build a nest egg for the future.

You should place 20 percent of the $200, or $40, into an emergency fund. Then if you overspend your grocery category by $20, you can go to your savings account and withdraw $20 from your emergency fund to replenish your groceries account.

The third part of your savings should be for emotional spending. This should be 20 percent of your savings. In this example, that is $40. The emotional spending category is for money that you don't have to worry about what you use it for. It is there for you to use to have fun. You might use it to take your family out for a night of fun or to go with your spouse to a fancy restaurant. Or you might use it to buy a new book you've been wanting to read. The emotional spending category is there to help satisfy your emotional needs.

Recommended Savings Distribution

Permanent	Emergency	Emotional
60%	20%	20%

You can be flexible with these percentages, but we feel that you should save some money in each category. One couple started out with 60 percent, 20 percent, and 20 percent but later decided to change it to 60 percent, 30 percent, and 10 percent. As you gain more experience using our recommended percentages, you may wish to vary the percentages according to your needs.

People sometimes ask us, "Suppose I have an extra $100 from a gift or some other source that I want to put into savings. Do I still follow your 60 percent, 20 percent, 20 percent rule?" We say yes. It is a good habit to get into, and it helps ensure that there will always be some savings in each category.

Another question people ask us is, "Do I need three savings accounts for these three savings categories?" No, no more than you need separate checking accounts for each expense category in your budget. Simply set aside three columns of your budget booklet for the three areas of savings.

An interest-bearing checking account works especially well with this method, as you can simply accumulate your savings from month to month in your checking account without losing interest. Then, when you feel you have accumulated enough savings, just write a check to transfer the money to your savings account.

Adequate savings are important, because they ensure that no matter what comes—sickness, loss of job, or natural disaster—you will be prepared and will be able to survive financially. In fact, we encourage you to save a year's supply of money.

You may find it hard to believe that you can save a year's supply of money, but you can, and it will give you a wonderful feeling of security. First, you should calculate how much that is. It is far less than your gross income. In fact, in most cases it is adequate to save the total of your fixed and variable expenses for one year. That is probably your house payment, utilities, car payment, insurance, groceries, and personal loans.

Once you have defined what a year's supply of money is for you, you can add a category to your budgeting booklet entitled Year's Supply of Money. As you receive each payroll or commission check, you can add money a little at a time to that category until you reach your goal.

How long will it take you to save a year's supply of money? That depends on you. What if it took three years, five years, or even ten years? How would you feel? Happy? Secure? Joyful? Pleased that you could accomplish what you once thought was impossible? Using your new budgeting system, you can do it. Then you will truly be rich on any income. We hope you will begin today.

12

The Will to Win

Now you know how to use the Financial Freedom Budgeting System. You know how to control your finances and how to avoid having your finances control you.

But knowledge is not always enough to motivate people. We have found that many people have failed so often at managing their money that they are afraid to try again, even with a system as simple and effective as the one presented in this book. For that reason, we would like to present a case study of a couple in deep financial trouble who learned to use the Financial Freedom Budgeting System to overcome their problems. This story is a true one, although the names of the couple have been changed. We hope that this story will help you spot some of the emotions and attitudes that lead to financial problems, and that it will help strengthen your commitment to successfully manage your money. The story is told in the couple's own words.

Irene: I won't go into the details of how Doug and I got into our financial problems. Suffice it to say that they began in our individual attitudes and habits before our marriage. Then from our honeymoon on, our financial situation grew worse and worse. We just seemed to have an undisciplined, disorganized financial life-style. As time passed, money was what we

needed to talk about most, but because the subject was so un-
pleasant and caused so much emotional stress and discord, we
talked about it less and less.

Doug: Because Irene was better at keeping track of the bills
and making out checks, she sort of inherited that task. I'd be
dead tired from work when we'd go to bed at night, and she'd
say, "Doug, we don't have enough money to pay the bills." My
blood pressure would rise, and as calmly as I could I'd say,
"Look, honey, this is no time to talk about money. It's late and
I'm tired. Things will work out. They always have before."

Somehow I couldn't accept the responsibility for our
money problems. But because Irene was the only one I could
blame, I'd get bad feelings toward her. I wouldn't tell her that,
but deep down that was the way I felt. I just couldn't understand
why we couldn't pay our bills even though I worked long and
hard every day.

Irene: At times when I'd be going over all the bills and trying to make things balance, I'd become depressed. I've always
been a happy person by nature, but the constant concern about
money was taking all the beauty from life. I am something of an
artist, but my creativity seemed to be vanishing, and love for
Doug was beginning to turn to resentment.

Doug: One reason I had fallen in love with Irene was her
carefree manner. She had laughed so easily and so often. It was
impossible to be around her without feeling lifted. But now she
seemed withdrawn much of the time. I sensed that part of the
problem was that she had to pay the bills and manage our
money alone. So we finally decided that I'd take over paying
the bills. I also felt that perhaps Irene wasn't getting the whole
financial picture and that I could distribute the money so that
things would work out better.

I could tell Irene was a bit hurt about this—that I was blaming her for our problems. But I felt that something had to be done.

I did a pretty fair job with the finances at first. But it was obvious that I wasn't as exacting in my financial record keeping as Irene was. Because of that, I decided that if she would go back to doing the clerical work, I'd point out what to pay and how much and when. Then we sort of drifted back to having her do the whole thing again.

We had these same problems for several years. Each year my wages would increase and we'd think that things would get better. With that hope, we'd charge a few things that we felt we needed. I don't know if it was inflation or the children needing more things as they got older; all I know is that more money didn't seem to solve anything. At times we'd get into some fairly heated arguments (we called them discussions) over money. One bright spot in all of this was that each year our house payments seemed more manageable as the amount I earned each year increased while our house payment stayed the same. The problem now was that the house was that the house was a bit too small for our four growing children.

On the way home from work one day, I spotted a house for sale on a street in an attractive part of town. The front door was open, so I went in. Somehow I knew as I walked from room to room that this was just the right house for our family. The next day at work I called the phone number on the real-estate sign. I was a little shocked at the price and asked if I could get the house for less. I was assured that because the family needed to sell it quickly that the price could probably be lowered a bit.

I didn't talk to Irene about buying the house right off. She had become so jumpy about money that she didn't even seem rational on the subject anymore. Because of that, I wanted to see just what the monthly payments would be and lay the whole thing out on paper before I approached her. The way I figured it, we could afford it if we tightened our belts in a few areas, and especially if we could get a good price for our present home.

Irene: When Doug told me what he wanted to do, I nearly died. The payments were so high that I could not believe he was serious. I could hardly restrain my bitterness as I shouted, "Doug, we can't afford it. We get letters and phone calls now telling us we are behind on this payment or that one. This whole financial mess is driving me out of my mind, and you don't even seem to care."

Doug: I was deeply hurt by Irene's remark. She wouldn't even listen to the way I had things figured out. Through the years I had become so sick of hearing her say "We can't afford it" that something inside me finally snapped. I got up from the table and walked out of the house.

As I walked down the sidewalk toward town, I could hear Irene saying over and over, "You don't even seem to care." But she was the one who didn't seem to care. All I wanted was a good home, and her only concern was money. I wanted to just keep on walking and never come back. I had worked hard; I was successful and appreciated at work. But at home Irene constantly reminded me that I was a failure. I'd made sacrifice after sacrifice for her and the children. I'd given up things that I wanted to do just so we could live comfortably. But was all that appreciated? Not a bit. I felt bitter that I wasn't able to keep up with my brothers and the guys I played golf with. I deserved to have things better.

Irene: When Doug left, I actually thought that he might not come back. I had seen the hurt look in his face. I was sorry, so deeply sorry for him. But I couldn't reach out to him because I hurt too much myself.

I wanted a nicer house as much as he did. I wanted to have people come into our home and admire our couch and our drapes. That's why I'd had the front room recarpeted while Doug was out of town at a seminar. I'd intended to get a less expensive carpet, but the salesman told me that I'd be sorry in a year or two if I did. He advised me to get the best and that in the long run it would actually be less expensive. The payments seemed reasonable when we spread them out over two years.

But don't misunderstand. We weren't really spendthrifts. We ate simple foods most of the time. We tried to budget our money and to keep track of how we spent it. We tried to save on our food bill, but we never knew exactly how much we spent each month on groceries. Sometimes we'd splurge and get some of the groceries we had agreed we could do without. That would throw everything else off, and then we'd have an even harder time with our money.

Doug: After I came back home, I picked up a book and went in the front room to read. Irene was in the kitchen cleaning up the dinner dishes. I usually helped, but not that night. I looked down at the carpet and resentfully considered that Irene hadn't even asked me whether we should buy it. She could decide things like that on her own, but I couldn't.

She came up behind me, put her hand on my shoulder, and said she was sorry. I just kept on reading and didn't reply. She went to bed. For the next half hour or so, I half read and half let my mind wander. As I considered our situation, I had a hard time holding back the tears. I'd never been so discouraged in my entire life. For the next three days I don't think we said more than fifty words to each other.

I felt that if Irene could sense how much the new house meant to me, she'd give in and say okay. Yet at the same time I knew we couldn't afford it. But we deserved the house. The children deserved it. They needed to feel good about where they lived. Why should they suffer just because their parents couldn't make it financially?

Irene: I could tell that Doug was deeply depressed. I'd try to approach him, but he'd turn me away. I guess I didn't try very hard; I was a little tired of trying. A month or so passed and Doug didn't say any more about the new house. We didn't talk about anything that really mattered. The week after Thanksgiving, while I was planning for Christmas, I asked Doug what we should get the children for Christmas. His answer was quick: "We can't afford anything."

It was then that we had our most bitter argument ever. Each of us threw at the other every resentment that we'd ever felt since the beginning of our marriage, and money was right in the center of every one.

Finally, Doug said that he thought our marriage was on quicksand and was about to go under. When he said that, I could scarcely stand—and without strength to do anything else I fell into his arms and wept uncontrollably. He held me tight, and finally in a surge of desperation he asked, "Oh, Irene, *what can we do?*"

Doug: Even at work, where my life had been fairly bright, things started to change. I had a run-in with my supervisor over some petty thing that I would have laughed at before. Finally, I guess he decided things couldn't go on the way they were. He called me in, and after we'd talked about who would win the upcoming bowl games, he took a deep breath and asked, "Doug, what's eating you lately? Things just aren't the way they used to be. What's wrong?"

He paused and kept looking at me. I lowered my eyes and had to control myself to keep from crying. We sat in silence for several seconds; then I looked back at him and said, "Sam, I just . . . well, things just aren't going well for Irene and me. We're not hitting it off like we used to, and our problems are eating away at me like cancer."

Then Sam told me he'd just learned that the company had hired a woman named Jan Ramsey to offer special services to the employees. He said she'd be over a department called Human Resource Development. He explained that among her duties would be helping employees with personal problems.

Sam said he'd call her and get me an appointment. He reached for the phone, but I stopped him and told him I didn't think I'd want to do that. He told me it was up to me, but that in his opinion it sure wouldn't hurt, and it might help.

That night after the ten o'clock news, I mentioned to Irene what had happened. She seemed quite concerned that I had been having trouble at work. When she learned about Jan Ramsey, she encouraged me to see her.

At 10:45 the next morning, I went to Jan Ramsey's office. As we got acquainted, I learned that she'd worked for my uncle while she was going to graduate school at the state university. She was easy to talk to, and an hour later, I had pretty well told her our story. She asked me if I could bring Irene with me to see her the next day at 2:00 P.M.

Irene: When Doug told me what had happened and about the appointment the next day, I felt a glimmer of hope. I told him maybe this could be the beginning of an answer. Doug replied, "Don't get your hopes up too high. She might just want to see the woman who was beautiful enough to win the love of someone as dashing as me."

I rolled up the dish towel and flipped it at him as he jumped backward. We were laughing. At the same instant we both realized that we hadn't laughed like that in a long time.

Doug: Irene and I spent an hour with Jan. Finally, she leaned forward and said softly, "Doug and Irene, you are two outstanding people. I've never met a couple who, in my opinion, are more perfectly suited to each other. You have a deep-rooted intellectual, emotional, and physical love for each other. But all that is being muddled up by one basic issue that is the source of all your major problems. That issue, as you are well aware, centers in your family finances. When you work out that problem, you'll be the happiest people in the world. If you don't work it out, you'll be the most miserable."

She then told us of a special seminar that her sister and her sister's husband had attended. She said her sister had raved about how it had helped them. She started looking through her desk drawer for some literature about it. I felt like saying, "Don't bother looking. Our problem isn't a seminar; it's a lack of money." She found the brochure and quickly leafed through it. Then she said, "Listen to what the brochure says: 'We guarantee that if you follow this method very sincerely and very carefully, you will be living within your means in ninety days.'"

I laughed and asked, "What is it, a course on how to rob a bank?"

Jan smiled and said, "That's what it sounds like, doesn't it? Actually, it is a special system for managing money. It's called the Financial Freedom Budgeting System, and from what my sister and her husband tell me, it really works.

"Why don't you give it a try? The company will pay the tuition. In fact, I've talked to the directors of the company about having the seminar taught to all our employees. They agreed. You know, you aren't the only ones who need this kind of help."

Irene: Doug's quick response was, "Don't worry about bringing the seminar here; just tell the boss to give us all a hundred-thousand-dollar raise!"

Jan laughed and said, "Yeah, I'll buy that!" Then she added, "But you know, more money isn't really the answer. Many people who make a hundred thousand dollars more than you do still have basically the same problem as you. Their money can't cover their bills any more than yours does."

I turned to Doug and said, "What have we got to lose?" His reply was, "Nothing, and the free tuition is just barely within our price range."

At the seminar, we started to learn the principles and techniques of the Financial Freedom Budgeting System. We sensed that technically the program would work, but we struggled with the psychological and emotional discipline we would need to carry it out. We were a bit skeptical that any lasting good would come of it.

When one of the seminar leaders, Jim, mentioned the word *budget,* I saw Doug shudder. To him and to me, that was now an emotion-packed word.

Jim, who was amazingly perceptive, paused and said, "What's wrong? Did I say something that bothered you?"

Doug replied, "No, go ahead."

Jim said, "Come on; we need to be honest with each other. What's the problem?"

Doug replied, "Well, I guess I expected something here that now I'm afraid I won't get."

Jim asked, "What's that?"

Doug said, "Well, I hoped to get some help. But when you said the answer is to budget, I knew the financial piano was playing the same old note: *budget, budget, budget!"*

Jim laughed and said, "Look, Doug, our Financial Freedom Budgeting System isn't a note, it's a symphony. Let us explain it and you'll see what I mean."

The answer seemed to calm Doug down for the time, and the seminar continued. During a rest break, Doug and I had a chance to talk privately with Jim.

I was shocked when Doug blurted out, "You make this all sound simple, but it isn't simple for us. We've tried budgeting before, but it isn't long before it all goes down the drain. Then we just sort of put out fires as they come up. We don't know how we can ever change that when we've got so many bills and not enough money."

Jim could see we were feeling part of the panic of our past financial pains. Reassuringly he said, "Doug and Irene, don't get me wrong. The answer is simple, but doing what needs to be done is as difficult a thing as you will ever do. As I said, this system isn't a single, easy-to-play note. It's a symphony, and symphonies don't come about easily. We'll teach you the notes, but you two will be the day-by-day musicians. To solve these problems, we won't be working with money as much as we will with emotions. We'll need to reach down right to the bottom of our hearts and decide what the foundation of happiness really is."

Doug: I felt some hope in what I was hearing, and I could tell that Irene did, too. I knew that our problems were deep, and I could sense that Jim understood.

Later when Jim talked about the commitment that would be needed to carry out the things we had discussed, he looked right at Irene and me and asked, "What about it? Are you willing to do it?"

I said, "Before I make any commitments, I want to tell you what my father once told me. He said not to drive the peg in too deep because you might have to pull it out with your teeth. I don't know yet exactly what you're asking us to commit to, but whatever it is, I want you to know that what Irene and I need and deserve is a larger home, not a budget. What is the use of living if all we have on our minds is a budget. I'm sick of hearing 'We can't afford it.' If a commitment means that, then I don't want any part of it."

Clint, the other seminar leader, had been listening intently. He finally said, "Let's get a few things straight. You do deserve that new house. If you can afford it, get it. If you can't, don't. You have worked hard. You have as much right to those big bedrooms, that spacious front room, those three bathrooms as anyone else does. You would feel proud to bring visitors into a home like that."

Then he paused and looked directly at me. He said, "Doug, you can have that house as your goal, or you can have peace of mind as your goal. The question you have to answer is which of the two will really be the thing that will bring you the most happiness. Which will cause Irene to love you more? Which will be the greatest source of emotional security for your children? The best thing you can give your children is a set of happy parents."

Irene: I could see that Clint was telling Doug what I had wanted to tell him. Oh, how I hoped Doug would understand.

Clint continued, "I don't know how much you earn, but if you decide to purchase that house on your projected earnings, you may indeed prove that you can afford it. But the emotional price that you and Irene may pay will be one that will never allow you to live a happy day within those walls."

Doug: For the next several seconds we all sat in silence. I looked at Irene, and I could see that her eyes were moist.

I drew in a deep breath. I hurt and felt good all at the same time. I hated to give in, but I wanted to let go. I wanted whatever was best for our family.

Clint spoke again: "Until you decide to do as we are suggesting, you will never really come to the starting line. You can't run a race without knowing where the starting line is. Only then can you know how far it is to the finish line, and if you don't know that, you won't know if you'll have the energy to finish what you start. Not knowing where you stand isn't happiness; it's the worst sort of misery."

Irene: Doug said, "I can see what you are saying, and I agree with you. But we've tried to budget before. Then we see what the neighbors have and what our brothers and sisters have, and that pulls us from our commitment. We just can't stick to it."

"I know, I know," Clint said with compassion. "It's a matter of discipline. It's a day-in and day-out pressure. Ideas flood us from commercials on television. We see people all around us buying this, that, and the other. It's a daily battle. But we have to drop out of the race that is being run by those around us. We must let them win the race to acquire luxurious comforts, and we must run the race that leads to peace of mind. Peace of mind is the greatest of all comforts. And you will find that our budgeting system really makes it all possible."

As I looked around the room, I noticed that all the couples were sitting a little closer to each other. I could tell that Doug's statement and Clint's reply had touched them. They had had similar experiences and feelings. It seemed that we were all ready to make the commitment to try the budgeting system for ninety days.

Doug: I looked at Irene, and she was looking back. I said, "We want to do it." Just saying that seemed to lift a burden from my shoulders.

Clint paused and looked at his watch. "It's time to stop," he said. "Now you are committed to getting control of your finances. Next week we will show you how our whole budgeting system works. Remember that during the week your assignment is to categorize last year's expenditures to see where your money went. Bring the results next time."

Irene: When we arrived home that night, the children were all in bed. Doug started reading the newspaper, and I began watching the closing scenes of my favorite television show. When Doug heard the TV go off, he lowered his paper and looked at me. We felt something between us that we hadn't felt in a long time. A wedge that had been driven between us was now gone.

I walked over and sat down at Doug's side. I touched his hand and said, "Doug, I love you." Tears welled up in his eyes. He held me in his arms and said, "And I love you, my dear, dear wife."

We sat there in silence for the next several minutes. To me, it was the happiest time of my life. I felt like Doug and I could conquer the world. And, as we sat there, I was amazed at how beautiful our furniture, drapes, and carpet appeared. It was as if we were in the most luxurious place on earth.

Doug: The next morning while I was shaving, I was thinking about the seminar. My first feeling was gratitude. But then a slight doubt entered my mind. How could we do it on our income? We owed so much, and we had so many bills. I knew that Jim and Clint could offer us advice that would help, but they couldn't give us money. And we needed money more than advice.

Irene: I worked on that history of our past year's expenditures every spare minute I got, and Doug helped at times. Whenever I showed him the results, he'd say, "Is that right? I didn't know we spent that much each month on that." It was exciting but a lot more difficult than I thought it would be. If we found our emotions rising, as they had so often when we discussed money before, we'd follow Jim and Clint's advice to instantly forgive each other and then go on. It seemed strange for the two of us to have a pleasant conversation about family finances.

Doug was pretty quiet as we drove to the seminar that week. As we walked from the car to the civic center, I said, "You seem a bit concerned. What's wrong?"

He replied, "I want desperately for this to work. But I just don't see how we can do it."

A few minutes later we were in the seminar. It was good to see all the other couples. Somehow we seemed like passengers on the *Titanic* who had all made it to the same lifeboat.

Jim stood and the seminar session began. "How do you all feel about the ninety-day commitment that you made to yourselves to follow the system?" he asked.

I didn't want to embarrass Doug, but I felt that his feelings needed to be expressed, so I said, "I think Doug has some concerns."

Jim asked, "Is that right, Doug?"

As Doug began to speak, I could tell the others were glad as he seemed to speak for the entire group. Doug said, "The other night I said that I wanted to do this. And I still do. But now that we've looked at what we spent last year and what we face this year and our present debts, I'm not so sure now that we can do it."

Jim replied, "I understand what you are saying. Suppose you let me say a few things, and then we will come back to what you've said.

Some people say you can do anything you really set your mind to do. Do you believe that is true, Doug?"

"I'm not sure," Doug replied.

Jim chuckled and continued, "I don't believe it myself. I don't believe I can run a four-minute mile no matter how much I set my mind to do so. Some things just aren't possible. But there are many things, things that matter a lot more than athletic feats, that can be done if we really decide to do them. Such things include losing weight, stopping smoking, or changing a bad habit. Living within our income is in this group. It can be done, and once you decide—I mean really decide—to do it, you can.

"Now, there aren't any commitments that last a lifetime. Some last a year, some a month, some a week, some a day, and some only hours or minutes. Commitments have to be renewed just like driver's licenses. Recommitment is what gives commitment a long-lasting life. Every time you go to the store or face any type of purchase, you'll need to recommit to your goal of living within your income. It will be tough, I know, but you can do it."

Doug: I remember wanting to tell Jim I knew that Irene and I could do it, but instead I asked, "Is it really worth it? I mean, is it worth that day-to-day struggle? Is it worth living without some of the good things of life?"

"Doug, you've just asked the key question," Jim replied. "You've pointed at the road that seems the more attractive one, namely, 'Buy whatever you want.' Very few can go down that road—no matter how rich they are—without forsaking the other road, which is 'financial peace of mind.' There are for almost all people more good things than their money can cover. That road is a road that so often doesn't have an end except a general area called hell. You know, Doug, you don't have to die to go to hell. Too much debt is an almost perfect hell."

Irene: Jim's words might have seemed harsh except that he smiled as he spoke and his eyes sparkled. He continued, "Doug, you look like you were probably an athlete while you were in school. If so, you know that getting ready for big games and playing them was not easy. It required a total commitment. But while you were making sacrifices by forgoing fun so as to get plenty of sleep, and while you were sweating and having the coach shout at you, it didn't seem bad because you were doing it for a purpose: You wanted to win. You wanted to win so badly you could taste it. And all that work and sweat didn't make your life miserable. It gave your life a purpose. Life is never more meaningful than when we want something that is made up of feelings rather than things.

"Doug, let me ask you something personal. The other night after you had said you'd do this, when you went home, did Irene seem prettier to you than she had in years? Did you look at her and want to hold her? Did you tell her with more sincerity than you had in a long time that you loved her?" As Jim was saying that, I looked over at Doug, and he looked at me. Doug smiled and said, "Have you been looking in our window or something?"

We all laughed. Then Jim looked very serious and said, "Doug and Irene, the other night you had a little bit of heaven in your home. You don't have to die to touch heaven. New couches, new drapes, new cars, and new homes can't make heaven. Heaven isn't things; it's feelings. And debt and unpaid bills can leave your heart pretty empty, even if you are driving a sports car to the country club."

Jim paused and asked, "Doug, have I said too much?"

Doug replied, "No, I needed to hear all you've said. I'll

need to hear it again and again. But right now I'm convinced, and I know Irene is too."

Jim continued, "Well, I just wanted to say all that because that's the foundation to the budgeting system you will learn to use tonight. Without that basic philosophy, the rest of what Clint and I have to teach you won't hold water."

There was a hush in the room as Jim finished his speech. I guess it was really more like a sermon. His words had touched us, and we knew that what he had said was right. Our own experiences with the misery of debt had taught us that. Without further discussion we were ready to go on. We wanted to follow the system and were eager to learn how, and we did.

Doug: It has been four years since Irene and I attended the Financial Freedom Budgeting Seminar. As time has passed, we have learned for ourselves that all the principles we learned there are true. Our family life now is filled with harmony. So often as I look at Irene, I recall the words of Clint, who asked, "When you look into your wife's eyes, do you see hearts or dollar signs?" I'm so grateful to say that I see hearts.

Irene: Doug has done well at his work. He has won the complete respect of all those who work with him. Promotions have come, and with them increases in salary.

We've taught our children the budgeting system, and we feel they will now be able to avoid the money problems that plagued us for so long.

By following the budgeting system and working together as a family, we have been able to afford many things that we formerly only dreamed about. But more important has been the fact that through saving money and staying current with all our obligations, we've had a continuing sense of security. Jim and Clint would be pleased to know that now we even have a year's supply of money.

Last Christmas we sat down and reminisced about our years together. We decided to write a Christmas letter to people who had helped us through the years—people like Sam at Doug's work, a schoolteacher who had helped our son through a difficult time, and a church leader who was there and cared when we needed him. And, of course, one special letter started this way:

Dear Jim and Clint:
We're writing this letter just to say thanks . . .

For information about a seminar on the Financial Freedom Budgeting System for your group, organization, or conference, contact Deseret Book, Attn: Financial Freedom Budget Seminars, P.O. Box 30178, Salt Lake City, Utah 84130.

Easy Money Management for Kids and Teens!

Young people today earn and spend more money than ever before. But often they have no idea how to manage their money or how to save it for the things they really want and need.

In *Rich on Any Allowance* they will learn to:
- set spending goals
- save money regularly
- limit impulse spending
- live within their means
- plan for the future

The authors promise: "If young people will follow the instructions in this book, they will have more of anything they want financially as long as they plan and work for it over time."

At last, here is a proven budget system designed especially for kids and teens, a system to help them achieve and enjoy financial freedom for the rest of their lives.

Order *Rich on Any Allowance* from your favorite bookstore or by calling toll-free 1-800-453-4532. (In Utah, call toll-free 1-800-662-3653. In the Salt Lake City area, call 534-1515.)

Appendix
Financial Worksheet and Budget Booklets

This appendix contains a worksheet to help you manage your finances as you follow the system described in this book. Use this form with chapter 4, "Calculating Income and Expense," and chapter 6, "Sharing the Burden and the Joy."

Following the worksheet are four copies of the Financial Freedom Budget Booklet. To assemble these booklets, cut the pages from the book along the dotted lines using a sharp pair of scissors or a razor blade. This will give you twelve loose pages. Take three of the pages, labeled A, B, and C in the lower right-hand corner. With the letters A, B, and C right-side up and facing up, put these three sheets on top of each other. Put the A sheet on the table first; then put the B sheet on top of the A sheet; finally, put the C sheet on top of the B sheet. Line up the staple marks in the center of the three sheets. Staple the sheets together along the center where the two staple marks appear. Finally, fold the top half of the booklet forward along the staple marks. Repeat for the other three booklets.

If you prefer not to cut this book, you can order a year's supply of the Financial Freedom Budget Booklet by calling toll free 1-800-453-4532. If you are in the state of Utah, call 1-800-662-3653. If you are in Salt Lake City, call 534-1515. Or, you can order with the form printed on the inside cover of the budget booklets included in this book.

BUDGET BUILDER

Commitment date to complete _____ Date completed _____

A. SPENDABLE MONTHLY *INCOME:*

	Current	Projected
Gross Monthly Income	$ _____	$ _____
Less Taxes (Income & FICA)	_____	_____
Total Spendable Monthly Income	_____	_____

B. BUDGET CATEGORY *EXPENSES:*

Budget Category	I Last 12 Months Totals	II Last 12 Mo. Ave. Per Month	III Next 12 Mo. Ave. Per Month	IV His $	V Her $
1. Allowances					
2. Automobiles					
3. Cleaning & laundry					
4. Clothing					
5. Contributions					
6. Debt payments					
7. Family Advancements					
8. Gifts					
9. Groceries					
10. Housing					
11. Insurance					
12. Investments					
13. Maintenance & improvements					
14. Medical, dental, drugs					
15. Miscellaneous, petty cash					
16. Recreation & entertainment					
17. Savings					
18. Subscriptions					
19. Utilities					
20. Vacation, trips					
21. _____					
22. _____					
23. _____					
24. _____					
25. _____					
TOTAL EXPENSES					

A. (Projected income) minus B. III (projected expenses) must equal $0.
Column III must equal the sum of columns IV and V.

FINANCIAL FREEDOM BUDGET BOOKLET

The Easy Budgeting System That Fits in Your Checkbook

CATEGORY	AMOUNT	FIRST PAYCHECK OR HIS	SECOND PAYCHECK OR HERS
1. Allowances	$		
2. Automobiles	$		
3. Cleaning & Laundry	$		
4. Clothing	$		
5. Contributions	$		
6. Debt payments	$		
7. Family advancements	$		
8. Gifts	$		
9. Groceries	$		
10. Housing	$		
11. Insurance	$		
12. Investments	$		

CATEGORY	AMOUNT	FIRST PAYCHECK OR HIS	SECOND PAYCHECK OR HERS
13. Maintenance & improvements	$		
14. Medical, dental, drugs	$		
15. Miscellaneous, petty cash	$		
16. Recreation & entertainment	$		
17. Savings	$		
18. Subscriptions	$		
19. Utilities	$		
20. Vacation trips	$		
21.			
22.			
23.			
24.			
25.			

TOTAL $ _____

NAME _____ MONTH _____ YEAR _____

BUDGET AMOUNT	$	BUDGET AMOUNT	$	BUDGET AMOUNT	$	BUDGET AMOUNT	$	BUDGET AMOUNT	$
ROLLOVER	$	ROLLOVER	$	ROLLOVER	$	ROLLOVER	$	ROLLOVER	$
BEGINNING BALANCE	$	BEGINNING BALANCE	$	BEGINNING BALANCE	$	BEGINNING BALANCE	$	BEGINNING BALANCE	$
CHECK #		CHECK #		CHECK #		CHECK #		CHECK #	

To order a 12-month supply of the Financial Freedom Budget Booklet or the book *Rich on Any Income: The Easy Budgeting System That Fits in Your Checkbook*, call one of the toll-free numbers or mail your order today.

PHONE ORDERS:
(Credit card customers only)

Outside Utah call toll free

1-800-453-4532

In Utah call toll free

1-800-662-3653

Local calls 534-1515

For information about a seminar on the Financial Freedom Budgeting System for your group, organization, or conference, contact:
Deseret Book, Attn:
Financial Freedom Budget Seminars, P.O. Box 30178,
Salt Lake City, Utah 84130.

Deseret Book EXPRESS

For a complete explanation of how to use the Financial Freedom Budgeting System (of which this booklet is a part), you'll want to read *Rich on Any Income: The Easy Budgeting System That Fits in Your Checkbook.*

MAIL ORDERS:
Mail to: Deseret Book Express, P.O. Box 30178, Salt Lake City, Utah 84130

	Quan	Price	Total
Financial Freedom Budget Booklet (12 booklets)		**$10.00**	
Rich on Any Income		$8.95	
Rich on Any Allowance (For kids and teens)		$8.95	
Subtotal			
Sales tax (where applicable) . . . . (For orders being shipped to the following states, add appropriate sales tax: Utah 5-3/4%, California 6%, Idaho 4%.)			
Total (No additional postage or handling required.)			

☐ Check enclosed   ☐ VISA   ☐ MasterCard   ☐ American Express

Card # _____ Exp. date _____

Name _____

Address _____

City, state, zip _____

BUDGET AMOUNT $ | ROLLOVER $ | BEGINNING BALANCE $ | CHECK #

B

CHECK #	BEGINNING BALANCE $	ROLLOVER $	BUDGET AMOUNT $
CHECK #	BEGINNING BALANCE $	ROLLOVER $	BUDGET AMOUNT $
CHECK #	BEGINNING BALANCE $	ROLLOVER $	BUDGET AMOUNT $
CHECK #	BEGINNING BALANCE $	ROLLOVER $	BUDGET AMOUNT $
CHECK #	BEGINNING BALANCE $	ROLLOVER $	BUDGET AMOUNT $

		BUDGET AMOUNT $	ROLLOVER $	BEGINNING BALANCE $	CHECK #
		BUDGET AMOUNT $	ROLLOVER $	BEGINNING BALANCE $	CHECK #
		BUDGET AMOUNT $	ROLLOVER $	BEGINNING BALANCE $	CHECK #
		BUDGET AMOUNT $	ROLLOVER $	BEGINNING BALANCE $	CHECK #
		BUDGET AMOUNT $	ROLLOVER $	BEGINNING BALANCE $	CHECK #

BUDGET AMOUNT $	ROLLOVER $	BEGINNING BALANCE $	CHECK #
BUDGET AMOUNT $	ROLLOVER $	BEGINNING BALANCE $	CHECK #
BUDGET AMOUNT $	ROLLOVER $	BEGINNING BALANCE $	CHECK #
BUDGET AMOUNT $	ROLLOVER $	BEGINNING BALANCE $	CHECK #
BUDGET AMOUNT $	ROLLOVER $	BEGINNING BALANCE $	CHECK #

FINANCIAL FREEDOM BUDGET BOOKLET

The Easy Budgeting System That Fits in Your Checkbook

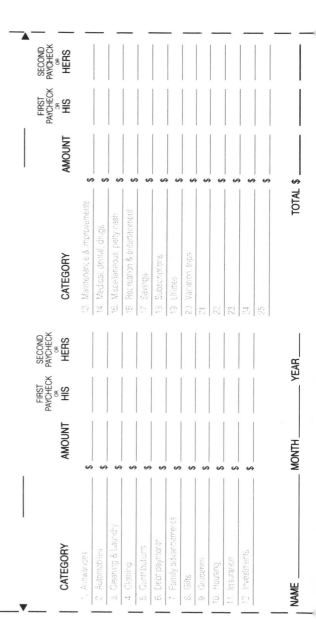

CATEGORY	AMOUNT	FIRST PAYCHECK OR HIS	SECOND PAYCHECK OR HERS
1. Allowances	$		
2. Automobiles	$		
3. Cleaning & Laundry	$		
4. Clothing	$		
5. Contributions	$		
6. Debt payments	$		
7. Family allowances	$		
8. Gifts	$		
9. Groceries	$		
10. Housing	$		
11. Insurance	$		
12. Investments	$		

CATEGORY	AMOUNT	FIRST PAYCHECK OR HIS	SECOND PAYCHECK OR HERS
13. Maintenance & improvements	$		
14. Medical, dental drugs	$		
15. Miscellaneous, petty cash	$		
16. Recreation & entertainment	$		
17. Savings	$		
18. Subscriptions	$		
19. Utilities	$		
20. Vacation trips	$		
21.	$		
22.	$		
23.	$		
24.	$		
25.	$		

NAME _____ MONTH _____ YEAR _____ TOTAL $ _____

To order a 12-month supply of the Financial Freedom Budget Booklet or the book *Rich on Any Income: The Easy Budgeting System That Fits in Your Checkbook*, call one of the toll-free numbers or mail your order today.

BUDGET AMOUNT $			BUDGET AMOUNT $		BUDGET AMOUNT $		BUDGET AMOUNT $
ROLLOVER $			ROLLOVER $		ROLLOVER $		ROLLOVER $
BEGINNING BALANCE $			BEGINNING BALANCE $		BEGINNING BALANCE $		BEGINNING BALANCE $
CHECK #			CHECK #		CHECK #		CHECK #

CHECK #	BEGINNING BALANCE $	ROLLOVER $	BUDGET AMOUNT $							
CHECK #	BEGINNING BALANCE $	ROLLOVER $	BUDGET AMOUNT $							
CHECK #	BEGINNING BALANCE $	ROLLOVER $	BUDGET AMOUNT $							
CHECK #	BEGINNING BALANCE $	ROLLOVER $	BUDGET AMOUNT $							
CHECK #	BEGINNING BALANCE $	ROLLOVER $	BUDGET AMOUNT $							

B

		BUDGET AMOUNT $	ROLLOVER $	BEGINNING BALANCE $	CHECK #

		BUDGET AMOUNT $	ROLLOVER $	BEGINNING BALANCE $	CHECK #

		BUDGET AMOUNT $	ROLLOVER $	BEGINNING BALANCE $	CHECK #

		BUDGET AMOUNT $	ROLLOVER $	BEGINNING BALANCE $	CHECK #

		BUDGET AMOUNT $	ROLLOVER $	BEGINNING BALANCE $	CHECK #

BUDGET AMOUNT $ | ROLLOVER $ | BEGINNING BALANCE $ | CHECK #

BUDGET AMOUNT $ | ROLLOVER $ | BEGINNING BALANCE $ | CHECK #

BUDGET AMOUNT $ | ROLLOVER $ | BEGINNING BALANCE $ | CHECK #

BUDGET AMOUNT $ | ROLLOVER $ | BEGINNING BALANCE $ | CHECK #

BUDGET AMOUNT $ | ROLLOVER $ | BEGINNING BALANCE $ | CHECK #

		BUDGET AMOUNT $	ROLLOVER $	BEGINNING BALANCE $	CHECK #
		BUDGET AMOUNT $	ROLLOVER $	BEGINNING BALANCE $	CHECK #
		BUDGET AMOUNT $	ROLLOVER $	BEGINNING BALANCE $	CHECK #
		BUDGET AMOUNT $	ROLLOVER $	BEGINNING BALANCE $	CHECK #
		BUDGET AMOUNT $	ROLLOVER $	BEGINNING BALANCE $	CHECK #

FINANCIAL FREEDOM
BUDGET BOOKLET

The Easy Budgeting System That Fits in Your Checkbook

CATEGORY	AMOUNT	FIRST PAYCHECK OR HIS	SECOND PAYCHECK OR HERS
1. Accessories	$		
2. Automobiles	$		
3. Cleaning & Laundry	$		
4. Clothing	$		
5. Contributions	$		
6. Debt payments	$		
7. Family advancements	$		
8. Gifts	$		
9. Groceries	$		
10. Housing	$		
11. Insurance	$		
12. Investments	$		

NAME _____ MONTH _____ YEAR _____

CATEGORY	AMOUNT	FIRST PAYCHECK OR HIS	SECOND PAYCHECK OR HERS
13. Maintenance & improvements	$		
14. Medical, dental drugs	$		
15. Miscellaneous, petty cash	$		
16. Recreation & entertainment	$		
17. Savings	$		
18. Subscriptions	$		
19. Utilities	$		
20. Vacation trips	$		
21.			
22.			
23.			
24.			
25.			

TOTAL $ _____

BUDGET AMOUNT	$		BUDGET AMOUNT	$		BUDGET AMOUNT	$		BUDGET AMOUNT	$
ROLLOVER	$		ROLLOVER	$		ROLLOVER	$		ROLLOVER	$
BEGINNING BALANCE	$		BEGINNING BALANCE	$		BEGINNING BALANCE	$		BEGINNING BALANCE	$
CHECK #			CHECK #			CHECK #			CHECK #	

To order a 12-month supply of the Financial Freedom Budget Booklet or the book *Rich on Any Income: The Easy Budgeting System That Fits in Your Checkbook*, call one of the toll-free numbers or mail your order today.

PHONE ORDERS:
(Credit card customers only)

Outside Utah call toll free
1-800-453-4532

In Utah call toll free
1-800-662-3653

Local calls   534-1515

For information about a seminar on the Financial Freedom Budgeting System for your group, organization, or conference, contact:
Deseret Book, Attn:
Financial Freedom Budget Seminars, P.O. Box 30178, Salt Lake City, Utah 84130.

Deseret Book
EXPRESS

For a complete explanation of how to use the Financial Freedom Budgeting System (of which this booklet is a part), you'll want to read *Rich on Any Income: The Easy Budgeting System That Fits in Your Checkbook.*

MAIL ORDERS:
Mail to: Deseret Book Express, P.O. Box 30178, Salt Lake City, Utah 84130

	Quan	Price	Total
Financial Freedom Budget Booklet (12 booklets)	___	$10.00	___
Rich on Any Income	___	$8.95	___
Rich on Any Allowance (For kids and teens)	___	$8.95	___
Subtotal			___

Sales tax (where applicable) . . . . ___
(For orders being shipped to the following states, add appropriate sales tax: Utah 5³/4%, California 6%, Idaho 4%.)

Total (No additional postage or handling required.) . . ___

□ Check enclosed   □ VISA   □ MasterCard   □ American Express

Card # _____   Exp. date _____

Name _____

Address _____

CHECK #	BEGINNING BALANCE $	ROLLOVER $	BUDGET AMOUNT $
CHECK #	BEGINNING BALANCE $	ROLLOVER $	BUDGET AMOUNT $
CHECK #	BEGINNING BALANCE $	ROLLOVER $	BUDGET AMOUNT $
CHECK #	BEGINNING BALANCE $	ROLLOVER $	BUDGET AMOUNT $
CHECK #	BEGINNING BALANCE $	ROLLOVER $	BUDGET AMOUNT $

B

BUDGET AMOUNT $								
ROLLOVER $								
BEGINNING BALANCE $								
CHECK #								

BUDGET AMOUNT $								
ROLLOVER $								
BEGINNING BALANCE $								
CHECK #								

BUDGET AMOUNT $								
ROLLOVER $								
BEGINNING BALANCE $								
CHECK #								

BUDGET AMOUNT $								
ROLLOVER $								
BEGINNING BALANCE $								
CHECK #								

BUDGET AMOUNT $								
ROLLOVER $								
BEGINNING BALANCE $								
CHECK #								

CHECK #	BEGINNING BALANCE	ROLLOVER	BUDGET AMOUNT
$	$	$	$

CHECK #	BEGINNING BALANCE	ROLLOVER	BUDGET AMOUNT
$	$	$	$

CHECK #	BEGINNING BALANCE	ROLLOVER	BUDGET AMOUNT
$	$	$	$

CHECK #	BEGINNING BALANCE	ROLLOVER	BUDGET AMOUNT
$	$	$	$

CHECK #	BEGINNING BALANCE	ROLLOVER	BUDGET AMOUNT
$	$	$	$

CHECK #	BEGINNING BALANCE	ROLLOVER	BUDGET AMOUNT
	$	$	$

CHECK #	BEGINNING BALANCE	ROLLOVER	BUDGET AMOUNT
	$	$	$

CHECK #	BEGINNING BALANCE	ROLLOVER	BUDGET AMOUNT
	$	$	$

CHECK #	BEGINNING BALANCE	ROLLOVER	BUDGET AMOUNT
	$	$	$

CHECK #	BEGINNING BALANCE	ROLLOVER	BUDGET AMOUNT
	$	$	$

FINANCIAL FREEDOM BUDGET BOOKLET

The Easy Budgeting System That Fits in Your Checkbook

CATEGORY	AMOUNT	FIRST PAYCHECK OR HIS	SECOND PAYCHECK OR HERS
1. Allowances	$		
2. Automobiles	$		
3. Cleaning & Laundry	$		
4. Clothing	$		
5. Contributions	$		
6. Debt payments	$		
7. Family advancements	$		
8. Gifts	$		
9. Groceries	$		
10. Housing	$		
11. Insurance	$		
12. Investments	$		

CATEGORY	AMOUNT	FIRST PAYCHECK OR HIS	SECOND PAYCHECK OR HERS
13. Maintenance & improvements	$		
14. Medical, dental, drugs	$		
15. Miscellaneous, petty cash	$		
16. Recreation & entertainment	$		
17. Savings	$		
18. Subscriptions	$		
19. Utilities	$		
20. Vacation trips	$		
21.			
22.			
23.			
24.			
25.			

TOTAL $ _____

NAME _____ MONTH _____ YEAR _____

BUDGET AMOUNT	$		BUDGET AMOUNT	$		BUDGET AMOUNT	$		BUDGET AMOUNT	$
ROLLOVER	$		ROLLOVER	$		ROLLOVER	$		ROLLOVER	$
BEGINNING BALANCE	$		BEGINNING BALANCE	$		BEGINNING BALANCE	$		BEGINNING BALANCE	$
CHECK #			CHECK #			CHECK #			CHECK #	

To order a 12-month supply of the Financial Freedom Budget Booklet or the book *Rich on Any Income: The Easy Budgeting System That Fits in Your Checkbook*, call one of the toll-free numbers or mail your order today.

PHONE ORDERS:

(Credit card customers only)

Outside Utah call toll free

1-800-453-4532

In Utah call toll free

1-800-662-3653

Local calls 534-1515

For information about a seminar on the Financial Freedom Budgeting System for your group, organization, or conference, contact:

Deseret Book, Attn:
Financial Freedom Budget
Seminars, P.O. Box 30178,
Salt Lake City, Utah 84130.

Deseret Book EXPRESS

For a complete explanation of how to use the Financial Freedom Budgeting System (of which this booklet is a part), you'll want to read *Rich on Any Income: The Easy Budgeting System That Fits in Your Checkbook.*

MAIL ORDERS:

Mail to: Deseret Book Express, P.O. Box 30178, Salt Lake City, Utah 84130

	Quan	Price	Total
Financial Freedom Budget Booklet (12 booklets)		$10.00	___
Rich on Any Income		$8.95	___
Rich on Any Allowance (For kids and teens)		$8.95	___
Subtotal			___
Sales tax (where applicable) (For orders being shipped to the following states, add appropriate sales tax: Utah 5³/₄%, California 6%, Idaho 4%)			___
Total (No additional postage or handling required.)			___

☐ Check enclosed ☐ VISA ☐ MasterCard ☐ American Express

Card # _____ Exp. date _____

Name _____

Address _____

BUDGET AMOUNT $ ROLLOVER $ BEGINNING BALANCE $ CHECK #

BUDGET AMOUNT $ ROLLOVER $ BEGINNING BALANCE $ CHECK #

BUDGET AMOUNT $ ROLLOVER $ BEGINNING BALANCE $ CHECK #

BUDGET AMOUNT $ ROLLOVER $ BEGINNING BALANCE $ CHECK #

BUDGET AMOUNT $ ROLLOVER $ BEGINNING BALANCE $ CHECK #

B

	BUDGET AMOUNT $	ROLLOVER $	BEGINNING BALANCE $	CHECK #
	BUDGET AMOUNT $	ROLLOVER $	BEGINNING BALANCE $	CHECK #
	BUDGET AMOUNT $	ROLLOVER $	BEGINNING BALANCE $	CHECK #
	BUDGET AMOUNT $	ROLLOVER $	BEGINNING BALANCE $	CHECK #
	BUDGET AMOUNT $	ROLLOVER $	BEGINNING BALANCE $	CHECK #

BUDGET AMOUNT $	ROLLOVER $	BEGINNING BALANCE $	CHECK #

BUDGET AMOUNT $	ROLLOVER $	BEGINNING BALANCE $	CHECK #

BUDGET AMOUNT $	ROLLOVER $	BEGINNING BALANCE $	CHECK #

BUDGET AMOUNT $	ROLLOVER $	BEGINNING BALANCE $	CHECK #

BUDGET AMOUNT $	ROLLOVER $	BEGINNING BALANCE $	CHECK #

CHECK #	BEGINNING BALANCE $	ROLLOVER $	BUDGET AMOUNT $
CHECK #	BEGINNING BALANCE $	ROLLOVER $	BUDGET AMOUNT $
CHECK #	BEGINNING BALANCE $	ROLLOVER $	BUDGET AMOUNT $
CHECK #	BEGINNING BALANCE $	ROLLOVER $	BUDGET AMOUNT $
CHECK #	BEGINNING BALANCE $	ROLLOVER $	BUDGET AMOUNT $